11/01

52 Quick Sketches

Paul McCusker has over 40 published works, including plays, novels, screenplays, radio dramas and lyrics. He is the writer and director of the Peabody Award-winning radio drama *Dietrich Bonhoeffer: The Cost of Freedom*.

Other works by the author

NOVELS:
You Say Tomato (with Adrian Plass)
Epiphany

GENERAL RESOURCE:
Youth Ministry Comedy & Drama: Better Than Bathrobes But Not Quite Broadway (with Chuck Bolte)
Playwriting: A Study In Choices & Challenges
The Ultimate Youth Drama Book

PLAYS:
The Case Of The Frozen Saints
The First Church Of Pete's Garage
The Revised Standard Version Of Jack Hill
The Performance of a Lifetime
Dear Diary
A Work In Progress
Camp W
Catacombs
Death By Chocolate
Family Outings
Father's Anonymous
Pap's Place
Snapshots & Portraits

MUSICALS:
The Meaning Of Life & Other Vanities (with Tim Albritton)
Shine The Light Of Christmas (with Dave and Jan Williamson)
A Time For Christmas (with David Clydesdale, Steve Amerson, Lowell Alexander)

ADVENTURES IN ODYSSEY NOVELS:
Strange Journey Back
High Flyer With A Flat Tire
Secret Cave of Robin Wood
Behind The Locked Door
Lights Out At Camp What-A-Nut
The King's Quest
Danger Lies Ahead
Point of No Return
Dark Passage
Freedom Run
Stranger's Message
Carnival of Secrets

VIDEOS:
Adventures In Odyssey: Once Upon An Avalanche
Adventures In Odyssey: Go West, Young Man

52 Quick Sketches

Paul McCusker

MONARCH
BOOKS

First published in 1992 by
Monarch Books, under the title *Fast Food,* and in 1999 by Gazelle Books as *52 Quick Sketches.* This edition published 2000 by Monarch Books, Concorde House, Grenville Place, Mill Hill, London NW7 3SA.

ISBN 1 85424 527 9

British Library Cataloguing Data

A catalogue record for this book is available from the British Library.

Designed and produced by
Gazelle Creative, Concorde House, Grenville Place, Mill Hill, London NW7 3SA.

Acknowledgements

Inasmuch as the idea of writing minute-long sketches with discussion questions was born out of my work for them, my heartfelt appreciation goes to Rob Parsons and Jonathan Booth at CARE for the Family; not only for the pity they took on me as a friend, but for their permission to adapt some of the *Family Matters* scripts for this collection.

I'm also grateful to Tony Collins for giving me this first opportunity.

And to my wife Elizabeth, without whom the various bits and bobs would not have been in place and a lot of people would have been scratching their heads in bewilderment … my deepest love.

Contents

Introduction

52 Quick Sketches is a collection of sketches created to stimulate thinking and discussion after being performed in as short a time as possible (approximately one minute) with as little rehearsal as possible (also approximately one minute – unless you want to take more time). This makes these sketches useful for a number of different reasons. Please bear with me while I state the obvious.

For one thing, they're useable just about anywhere: as sermon enhancers for worship services, house group or youth meetings, or the odd party where the mere mention of *Pictionary* might cause a mass exodus.

Because they're useable just about anywhere, I didn't elaborate on specific settings or acting requirements. You can do as much or as little as your time and budget allow. Make two chairs into a living room or build an elaborate set – it's whatever you make of it.

Likewise, your actors may perform these spontaneously or rehearse them for weeks prior, depending on their ability and interest. For those who couldn't give a toss about drama, these sketches can be simple games. For others who've been waiting for that big break to teach Kenneth Branagh a thing or two, they can be catalysts for creativity and, perhaps, depth of performance. My intention was to be as flexible as possible without compromising effectiveness.

The skit subjects are varied but, by the very nature of their presentation, aren't intended to be some vain Christian attempt to provide conclusive answers (at least that wasn't *my* intention). They're merely glimpses of particular characters and situations that may be familiar to your audience. After these glimpses, you may guide your audience into some lively discussions through the questions found after each sketch. I tried to pack a little bit of everything in here – from the struggles of modern youth to religious conflicts to the normal everyday problems most adults face as workers and parents. The skits are organised alphabetically by themes and topics for your convenience. As for the styles: they're as varied as the topics. You'll find slice-of-life drama, comedy, monologues, even the absurd.

By the way, certain terms in the dialogue may be unfamiliar. The most commonly used notations are the pause and beat. A pause is exactly what you'd suspect – a momentary stop in the flow of dialogue allowing the character to think about, take action or react to what's happening. A beat, on the other hand, not only stops the flow of dialogue for a moment, but re-directs it through a change in subject, tone of voice, line delivery or action. Exactly how *long* a pause or beat may last depends on the character, dialogue and overall direction.

Novice performers may be intimidated by any amount of time on the stage that isn't filled with words (the old 'just let me say my lines and get off the stage' mentality). More seasoned performers understand the importance of pauses and beats and use them to full advantage: to heighten the drama or draw out bigger laughs. It should be noted that none of the pauses or beats are intended to reach *Pinteresque* proportions.

I purposefully left out a few terms, too ('Stage Left' and 'Stage Right' for example). I did this to avoid confusion for those churches or meeting places where 'Stage Left' and 'Stage Right' don't exist, or may exist but need to be altered to make the sketch work. The characters in these sketches are either on stage when the sketch begins, or enter and/or exit from wherever the director decides. In lieu of the traditional 'blackout' at the end of the sketch, I've simply asked actors to 'freeze' in position while the group leader takes control of the meeting. This 'freeze' should remain in place until it's clear that the sketch is over after which the performers may walk off stage. Once again, flexibility within a cross-section of needs was my principal concern.

It's my sincere hope that these sketches will be fun and helpful to you as you explore new ways of bringing life into your group or church experience.

Paul McCusker
1999

NORMAL

THE TOPIC/THEME
Adjusting to change

THE SITUATION
Two women share some tea and the changes in their lives.

THE CHARACTERS
PATRICIA
RACHEL

THE PLACE
A home.

THE SKETCH

[A WIFE AND FRIEND HAVING TEA]

PATRICIA More tea?

RACHEL No, thank you. I want you to finish what you were saying.

PATRICIA What was I saying?

RACHEL About the way things have been.

PATRICIA Oh, yes. [RESUMING] Well, you know, John and I got married and we had all the normal problems in our first year. But we got through them. We came up with a solid plan for ourselves.

RACHEL I remember some of that. You gave me lots of advice before I married Terry.

PATRICIA We settled into a good marriage, John and I. We were happy. Then—surprise—I got pregnant and had Jennifer. And we had to re-adjust a bit and I thought it would be all right—everything would get back to normal.

RACHEL Uh huh.

PATRICIA Then John was promoted and transferred and we had to get used to a new area and...and then I had little David and we moved back again and...well, I knew we'd work it out once everything settled down and got back—

RACHEL —to normal. Right.

PATRICIA And I used to get so frustrated because things weren't going according to plan. Until I finally realised something very important.

RACHEL What?

PATRICIA Things never got back to normal. And they never will.

[THEY FREEZE IN POSITION AS THE DISCUSSION LEADER ENTERS. AFTER AN APPROPRIATE TIME, THEY EXIT]

THE QUESTIONS

1. Can you sympathise with Patricia? How? React to the conclusion she makes about things never getting back to normal.

2. Do you face periods of change in your life? Do you consider change good or bad? How do you cope with change when it comes?

3. What does the Bible say about change? What is the Christian expected to do when faced with change? Should we ever desire things to get back to 'normal' once they've changed?

GOD'S JUDGEMENT

THE TOPIC/THEME
AIDS & God's Judgement

THE SITUATION
We're told how AIDS has affected a man and his relationship with God.

THE CHARACTERS
A SPEAKER (could be male or female)

THE PLACE
Anywhere.

THE SKETCH

[SPEAKER ENTERS, STOPS CENTRE]

SPEAKER

A friend of mine is in the hospital. He has AIDS. It's quite advanced. I've been visiting him regularly—just to show him that I care and... I suppose I'm hoping that he might get to know Jesus before... you know.

It's been difficult. He wants to know God. He asks a lot of questions. You know, about the relationship between God and Jesus and why things happened the way they did. He's genuinely interested. He's searching. But... something has been holding him back from making any sort of commitment.

I couldn't figure it out. Then I realised that the reason he's hesitant about accepting Jesus is that he's not sure of what to make of Christians. See, the last time he went to church, he heard a sermon saying that AIDS was God's judgement on homosexuals. That was hard for him to take—the idea that God had singled out homosexuals—apart from all other sinners—to be judged like that. It didn't make sense to him.

Later, when he was tested HIV positive and told his family, the ones who wouldn't have anything to do with him were the Christians. They simply ignored him... and his situation. Again, he was confused. He never expected them to approve of his lifestyle, but he didn't expect that kind of rejection either.

He once heard a preacher say something about 'hating the sin but loving the sinner'. Unfortunately, all he ever saw was the 'hating the sin' part.

And that's what I'm up against.

How do I explain the love of Jesus to someone who has only known chastisement and rebuke from those who claim to know Jesus best?

I don't know what to say.

What would *you* say?

[THE SPEAKER EXITS. THE DISCUSSION LEADER ENTERS]

THE QUESTIONS

1. Answer the Speaker's question.

2. Is AIDS God's judgement on homosexuality? Explain your answer, using Bible verses, if possible.

3. What should be the Christian response to homosexuality and AIDS? Can you support your answer with verses from the Bible?

4. Do you know anyone who is suffering from AIDS? If so, how did you react when you were told? How are you helping the sufferer?

WORDS

THE TOPIC/THEME

Arguing

THE SITUATION

Two people argue about their arguing techniques.

THE CHARACTERS

FIRST PERSON

SECOND PERSON

[It could be a parent and child, siblings, or two friends]

THE PLACE

A room.

THE SKETCH

[FIRST AND SECOND PERSON ENTER IN THE MIDDLE OF AN ARGUMENT]

FIRST PERSON That's it. I don't have anything left to say.

SECOND PERSON No way! I'm not finished talking.

FIRST PERSON You aren't, but I am. I'm...I'm going for a walk [MUMBLES] or something.

SECOND PERSON No. It isn't fair. You can't close up on me now.

FIRST PERSON Close up? When did I get a chance to be *open*? I couldn't get a word in edgeways.

SECOND PERSON I've given you plenty of chances.

FIRST PERSON Yeah? When? Everytime I started to talk, you interrupted. When I tried to tell you how I felt, you showed me how I was wrong to feel that way.

SECOND PERSON Okay, then tell me. Right now. Tell me what you feel.

FIRST PERSON [PAUSE] Forget it. You'll have some clever remark to make or...make me feel stupid. I don't care anymore. I'm tired of this.

SECOND PERSON Oh come on.

FIRST PERSON Come on nothing. This is a waste of time. You're smart—a lot smarter than me—and I can't argue with you. You're good with words. You say everything right. And I can't. So I'm doing the only thing I can think to do.

SECOND PERSON What?

FIRST PERSON Leave.

[FIRST PERSON EXITS. SECOND PERSON REMAINS, FUMING]

SECOND PERSON That was a stupid thing to do.

[SECOND PERSON EXITS AS THE DISCUSSION LEADER ENTERS]

THE QUESTIONS

1. What was the fundamental problem with the two people in this sketch?

2. Try to relate to the first person in this sketch. Have you ever tried to discuss/argue with someone who was better with words than you (or wouldn't give you the chance to talk)? How did you feel about it? What did you ultimately do?

3. Try to relate to the second person in this sketch. Do you think you were right or wrong? How did you feel towards the first person—especially when he/she walked out before the argument was resolved? How might you become a better listener in a situation like this?

4. Read Psalms 19:14 and 39:1; Proverbs 15:1 and 23; and James 3:7–12 and apply to the situation in this sketch.

ABOUT CHURCH

THE TOPIC/THEME
Attitudes: church

THE SITUATION
Two girls make some observations at the start of a church service.

THE CHARACTERS
RACHEL
SHARON

THE PLACE
A church service.

THE SKETCH

[SITTING NEXT TO EACH OTHER, RACHEL IS TALKING TO THE AUDIENCE WHILE SHARON WATCHES THE PEOPLE IN THE SERVICE. EACH ONE SEEMS TO BE OBLIVIOUS TO WHAT THE OTHER IS SAYING]

RACHEL I like this church. I actually look forward to coming here to worship.

SHARON [NUDGES RACHEL, IMPRESSED WITH WHAT SHE SEES] Oh, Rachel—look at that, will you? Jason. Oooo!

RACHEL I like the people. They seem to share a genuine love for each other.

SHARON [DISAPPOINTED] Aw...never mind. He's talking to Karen. What's he see in her? She's such a cow.

RACHEL You can feel the spirit when you come into the building.

SHARON She's wearing that jumper again. Tht makes eight Sundays in a row. I wonder if she ever washes it?

RACHEL There's a true sense of praise in the music.

SHARON I suppose she's going to play guitar again this morning. She's given a whole new meaning to 'Make a joyful noise...'

RACHEL The teaching is solid, too. I always leave having learned something new about God.

SHARON Who's preaching this morning? I hope it isn't Dave. He doesn't know when to stop. Half the time I don't understand what he's on about.

RACHEL After the service, we have a time of fellowship when I feel like I can get closer to the people here. Last week, a handful of us prayed together.

SHARON I hope they have someone serving coffee who knows how to do it. They make it so *strong*.

Sue keeps trying to get me to volunteer to serve but I don't have time. That time after the service is the only chance I get to talk to everybody.

RACHEL It's a good opportunity to meet visitors and make them feel welcome.

SHARON [NUDGING RACHEL AGAIN] Ooo, look what just walked in. I haven't seen him before. Do you think he's new? Crumbs, I'll have to get to him before Karen does. She'll have her talons in him in no time!

RACHEL [SIGHS CONTENTEDLY] I really do love this church.

SHARON [TURNS TO RACHEL] Huh?

RACHEL This church—I like it.

SHARON Oh. Yeah. So do I. What isn't there to like?

[THEY FREEZE IN POSITION AS THE DISCUSSION LEADER ENTERS. AT AN APPROPRIATE TIME, THEY EXIT]

THE QUESTIONS

1. Summarise the differences between Rachel's attitudes and Sharon's attitudes about church. Which attitudes most closely resemble your own?

2. Why does Rachel go to church? Why does Sharon go to church? List 5 reasons why *you* go to church.

3. What do you like about church? What do you dislike about it? If you could change anything about church—to make it a better experience for yourself—what would you change?

4. How much do the people of the church affect your desire to go to church? Do you think someone ever goes to church—or stays away—because *you're* there?

SINGLE GIRLS

(Adapted with permission from CARE for the Family's *Family Matters*)

THE TOPIC/THEME
Being single

THE SITUATION
Two girls lament their singleness on a Friday night.

THE CHARACTERS
JO
ANNE

THE PLACE
Jo's and Anne's flat.

THE SKETCH

[A LIVING ROOM. TWO WOMEN PREPARING FOR THEIR 'BIG' FRIDAY NIGHT. ANNE IS SITTING ON A CHAIR, ARMS CROSSED DEFIANTLY]

JO [ENTERS WITH CHINESE TAKE-AWAY] I've got the take-away. Did you pick up the video?

ANNE No, I didn't. I'm rebelling.

JO You're what?

ANNE Rebelling. [BEAT] Jo, you're a wonderful flatmate, but if I spend another Friday night watching videos and eating Chinese with you, I may become suicidal.

JO Oh... [TRYING TO APPEASE] It's a little late about the Chinese, but we don't have to watch videos.

ANNE [NOT BELIEVING IT] Oh?

JO We could do something else.

ANNE Yeah—like what? A game of *Monopoly*? Rinse tights? I'm nearly 30 years old, Jo! There *must* be something better.

JO You could have gone out with Donald, you know—he's been after you for quite awhile.

ANNE I'd rather rinse tights.

JO What's wrong with Donald?

ANNE Nothing—except he's not my type. There's nothing about him that I find attractive.

JO He's not so bad.

ANNE It's not that he's *bad*, it's only that... well, somehow, going out with him would be like admitting defeat. [BEAT] I don't understand it, Jo. We're two attractive women. We take care of ourselves. We're intelligent. Fun to be with. But—

JO None of those things seems to attract men.

ANNE Exactly. What are we doing wrong?

JO [PAUSE] I don't know. [BEAT, BRIGHTLY] So—what video will it be?

ANNE [THOUGHTFULLY] Perhaps I *should* ring Donald.

[THEY FREEZE AS THE DISCUSSION LEADER ENTERS. AFTER A MOMENT, THEY EXIT]

THE QUESTIONS

1. Do you relate to either character in this sketch? If so, which one? How do you relate to her?

2. Anne wonders what she and Jo are doing wrong so that they can't seem to find men they're interested in. Answer her question.

3. What advice would you give to Anne, Jo and many other singles who are looking for the right person but can't find him/her?

4. How does Christian faith come into play in a situation like this? Do you believe that God has one person specially picked out for you? What does the Bible say about dating?

5. Do you think Anne should call Donald? Why or why not? If you think she should, do you think it would be fair to Donald (to go out with him when she's not attracted to him)?

TRAMPS

THE TOPIC/THEME
Charity

THE SITUATION
A man reacts when a friend gives money to a tramp.

THE CHARACTERS
COLIN
MARK
[Note: with some slight alterations, these characters could be played by women.]

THE PLACE
A street.

THE SKETCH

[MARK ENTERS, WALKING WITH PURPOSE. COLIN FOLLOWS A BEAT LATER AS IF TRYING TO CATCH UP, WHICH HE DOES]

COLIN Mark—wait. Mark.

MARK [STOPS, IRRITABLY] Come on, we're going to be late.

COLIN What's wrong?

MARK I wish you hadn't done that.

COLIN What—give money to that man back there?

MARK It only encourages them to sit around begging. The city's over-run with them.

COLIN What was I supposed to do?

MARK Just walk past.

COLIN But...he spoke to me.

MARK Of course he did. They all do. And the trick is to ignore them—don't make eye contact or you're done for. That's where they get you. The eyes.

COLIN Oh.

MARK Give them money and you're telling them you approve of them sitting on their bums begging.

COLIN Is that what I'm telling them?

MARK It is. Loud and clear. They could work if they wanted to—but why should they when there're people like you supporting them?

COLIN I hadn't thought about that.

MARK It's people like you who are contributing to the massive unemployment in this country, you know.

COLIN I was only trying to help.

MARK Now you know better. Now, come on, we're going to be late for the evangelism rally.

[THEY EXIT AS THE DISCUSSION LEADER ENTERS]

THE QUESTIONS

1. Do you agree with Mark's attitude about the poor? Why or why not?
2. Does Mark's attitude reflect the thinking of a lot of people today? How? Have you seen these attitudes at work first-hand?
3. If you were Colin, what would you have done in that same situation? When you pass by someone begging for money, how do you feel? How do you react?
4. What is the Bible's perspective on giving to the poor? (Read Matthew 5:42, 38–42, 25:40; James 2:15–17 for starters.)

CONTRASTS

THE TOPIC/THEME
Christian experience

THE SITUATION
We enter the private thoughts of a church member as he/ she listens to a sermon.

THE CHARACTERS
MINISTER
INDIVIDUAL

THE PLACE
A church service.

THE SKETCH

[A MINISTER ENTERS AND READS FROM THE BIBLE ON A PODIUM. NEARBY, WE HEAR THE THOUGHTS OF A SEATED INDIVIDUAL—OVERLAPPING, THOUGH NOT NECESSARILY AS A REACTION TO—WHAT THE MINISTER IS SAYING]

MINISTER There are fundamental promises from God that each one of us can claim for ourselves. Then we can live a victorious life in Christ as His blood cleanses us from sin.

INDIVIDUAL I don't understand why I fight with the same problems over and over again.

MINISTER You can expect God's presence in your life.

INDIVIDUAL I want to change, I want to live the way God wants me to, but I feel so alone in it. I wonder if He's there at all and—if He is—why isn't He helping me more?

MINISTER God will keep you and give you strength for His service.

INDIVIDUAL I mean, I'm so weak in things I figure I should've worked through by now.

MINISTER You can expect answers to your prayers.

INDIVIDUAL And when I pray—it feels like something isn't connecting. I can't figure out what I'm doing wrong. Maybe I don't have enough faith. I thought I did. I try.

MINISTER God will work miracles in your life.

INDIVIDUAL I see things happening in other people's lives. They seem so...so close to God. And I'm not. And I don't understand why. What do they have that I don't?

MINISTER God will fill your life with love.

INDIVIDUAL Sometimes I resent them. When they try to help me, I accuse them of being self-righteous. I act like they couldn't possibly understand how I feel—what a struggle it is for me.

MINISTER God honours obedience as you surrender to Him.

INDIVIDUAL They make it seem so easy. It's as if their Christianity fits them like a glove. So snug, so comfortable. I'm an odd size, I suppose.

MINISTER God wants you to succeed and prosper.

INDIVIDUAL I just can't seem to get it right. I make the same mistakes over and over and can't get ahead. It's miserable.

MINISTER God wants us to live in peace and unity.

INDIVIDUAL And I'm finding it harder and harder to want to go to church. I feel like a hypocrite. Oh sure, I can put on a good front and make it look like I'm doing all right—but I know better. I'm not fooling God, I'm sure. I look around at everyone else and wonder if any of them feel like I do. Probably not. So I resent them all over again.

MINISTER God wants you to be a witness for Him. [EXITS]

INDIVIDUAL Maybe I should give up. Maybe being a Christian is only good for some people. It's certainly not something I feel comfortable talking about. I mean, how could I explain it to others when it doesn't seem real to me? I...I feel such a failure.

[PAUSE. EXITS. GROUP LEADER TAKES CONTROL]

THE QUESTIONS

1. Are the statements made by the minister true? If not, which ones would you disagree with? Can you apply the things the preacher said to your own Christian experience?

2. Can you empathise with the individual in this sketch? In what ways? What feelings did he/she share that are closest to your own feelings? How do you reconcile your own frustrations and inadequacies with the biblical expectations for the Christian experience?

3. How do you cope with times of doubt and failure as a Christian?

4. What advice would you give to the Individual in this sketch about:

   Battling against the same sins again and again
   An inability to change
   Ineffectual prayer
   Comparing our spirituality to others
   Lack of peace
   Confusion
   Feeling like a hypocrite
   Feelings of failure

WHERE IT BEGINS

THE TOPIC/THEME
Christians & Affairs

THE SITUATION
Michael and Anne, two Christians, talk after a Bible study.

THE CHARACTERS
ANNE
MICHAEL

THE PLACE
Outside someone's home where a Bible study takes place.

THE SKETCH

[MICHAEL ENTERS, MOVING ACROSS STAGE AS IF HE JUST LEFT A HOUSE AND IS WALKING TO HIS CAR. ANNE RACES TO CATCH HIM UP. THEY ARE BOTH CARRYING BIBLES]

ANNE Michael?

MICHAEL [STOPS, TURNS TO HER, PLEASANTLY] Hello, Anne.

ANNE [AWKWARDLY] I...I wanted to thank you—for what you said inside—about perseverance.

MICHAEL [MODESTLY] Uh, thank you.

ANNE It was timely for me. It spoke...I mean, it's something I've been struggling with.

MICHAEL Who doesn't? Keeping the faith isn't always easy. At least, I don't think it is.

ANNE But it was nice to hear someone else admit that. I struggle a lot, you know. My husband isn't a Christian.

MICHAEL You mentioned that in prayer.

ANNE [EMBARRASSED] Did I? Oh, I hope I don't do that too much. Nothing worse than someone bleating on and on about the same thing.

MICHAEL You don't bleat.

ANNE It's only that...I feel lonely sometimes—for Christian company.

MICHAEL You have us.

ANNE Yeah, but...talking to a group isn't the same as talking to one person who understands. You...you're good at that. Understanding, I mean. You listen.

MICHAEL [SHRUGS] I try to.

ANNE It's nice to know. When I'm at home—when it feels empty—I look forward to our study group. To seeing...everybody. That night you prayed with me meant a lot.

MICHAEL It was important for me, too.

ANNE Was it?

MICHAEL Yeah...my wife isn't so keen on praying together. She says it makes her feel embarrassed. Funny, really.

ANNE At least you can talk to her about it. I can't even bring the subject up without my husband getting angry.

MICHAEL That's sad. [PAUSE] Would you like to pray now?

ANNE [EMBARRASSED] Out here in the street?

MICHAEL No...my car's just over there.

ANNE I'd like that...very much.

[THEY EXIT TOGETHER AS THE DISCUSSION LEADER TAKES OVER]

THE QUESTIONS

1. Michael and Anne are two caring Christians who decide to pray together. In itself, there isn't anything questionable about that activity. Why do you think this sketch was placed under the 'Christians & Affairs' category?

2. How do affairs begin (Christian or not)? How might Michael and Anne be setting themselves up for potential problems? Under what circumstances would you be tempted to seek the company of someone of the opposite sex?

3. Both Michael and Anne make seemingly innocent statements about their respective spouses. What did they say? What does this tell you about their relationships with their spouses? How might this make their praying together fertile ground for an affair?

4. What advice would you give to Michael and Anne about praying together privately? Should a man and woman who are not married to each other pray together privately? What are the benefits of members of the opposite sex praying together? What are the problems?

5. What advice would you give anyone who is married to someone who he or she feels is spiritually 'incompatible'?

CHRISTMAS FEELINGS

THE TOPIC/THEME
Christmas

THE SITUATION
We hear six monologues reflecting various feelings about Christmas. (These monologues can be used separately or all together with the speakers assembled on stage at the same time.)

THE CHARACTERS
Six speakers

THE PLACE
Anywhere.

THE SKETCH

SPEAKER 1.

I'm not what you'd call a very deep person, you know? I don't 'read between the lines' much, so to speak. I take things at face value. Life happens and you simply have to deal with it. To some people, that makes me a pragmatist. To others, I'm a superficial dolt. Doesn't matter. [PAUSE] But I have been thinking about one thing...Over the past few years I've been bugged whenever we get to what they happily call the 'holiday season'. Used to be that time in December lasting through to Christmas Day. Now it's any time past the summer bank holiday. Funny. When I was growing up, it used to start whenever the Christmas catalogues arrived. [BEAT, REMEMBERING] That was the way to tell Father Christmas what we wanted—to choose from the pages in the catalogues—[SIGHS] what I wouldn't give to capture that sense of joy...anticipation... *wonder* again.

I'm sure you have this all figured out—that gnawing, aching, bittersweet feeling I get whenever Christmas comes around—an emptiness, sort of. I guess I'm not deep enough to know what it is. But I know this: it gets worse every year. You know? I do all the right things at Christmas, but I'm feeling it less and less.

A friend of mine says it's just growing up. I said: 'are you kidding? Growing up at *my* age?'

He said 'Yeah. Good feelings at Christmas are always the last to go.' The last vestige of innocence, I guess.

I said: 'What about the Christmas spirit, huh? The Christmas spirit is for all ages!'

He said: 'Yeah? Have you been to the *town centre* lately?'

[BEAT] He had me on that one.

SPEAKER 2.

I've been trying to sort out what makes Christmas *Christmas*. I know it has a lot to do with children, that's for sure. When *I* was a child, do you think I asked myself if I thought I'd be in the Christmas spirit this year? Not a chance. It simply seemed to...*happen*. Instinctively. I didn't have to think about it or psyche myself up or worry about it. Christmas brought its own optimism and warmth and hope...I don't know how I lost that. Being a child is definitely part of it, though.

SPEAKER 3.

Do you want to know what *really* got me ready for Christmas? Now don't laugh.

Television.

With all those musicals and specials and films and adverts and...well, you know. All those songs, the spectacle, families gathered around the Christmas trees...that's how it's *supposed* to be. [PAUSE] But it isn't...only on television.

I wish my life was more like a television programme.

SPEAKER 4.

Christmas will only ever be what I make of it—and only as real as I want it to be.

SPEAKER 5.

I hear the songs...the memories come...the traditions fall into place. And then that ache, that crowded loneliness. An expectation that cannot be met. What is it? And why does it happen mostly at Christmas? I ask you! Be reasonable. What is it about Christmas that seems to act as some kind of amplifier of what we're feeling...or *not* feeling. If we're happy, Christmas makes us happier. If we're lonely, it makes us lonelier. If we're apathetic, it makes us...apatheticer. [BEAT] Don't bother to look it up. [RESUMING] It's as if Christmas is that one time of year when we have to come face-to-face with what we're really feeling. Sometimes...that's a terrible thing to have to do. [PAUSE] Because some of us are *really* hurting.

SPEAKER 6.

So what does that leave me with? Traditions, memories...and each other. I suppose the rest of it is just a matter of faith. [PAUSE/BEAT] But then—come to think of it—that's all it was when I was a kid—a matter of faith. Looking through the eyes of innocence...and seeing something more beyond the disguises, the activities, and the diversions...something more.

It's been there all along...we just have to remember how to see it.

[THE SPEAKERS EXIT AS THE DISCUSSION LEADER ENTERS]

THE QUESTIONS

1. Which speaker most closely articulates your feelings about Christmas? If none of them do, express your own feelings. What makes you feel Christmassy?

2. Define the 'spirit of Christmas'. How can we get past the 'commercialism' of Christmas to discover the true spirit?

3. There seems to be a link between the speaker's joy of child-like innocence and Christmas. Do you agree or disagree? Can adults recapture that feeling? How?

4. Rate the following in order of contribution to your Christmas spirit:

   Family traditions
   Christmas decorations
   Television programmes
   Shopping
   Gift-wrapping
   Church services or activities
   Children
   Opening presents

   What others would you add to this list?

5. Explain one family tradition you enjoy every Christmas.

DIVISIONS

THE TOPIC/THEME
Church divisions

THE SITUATION
Two Christians try to reconcile conflicting points of view.

THE CHARACTERS
FIRST PERSON
SECOND PERSON

THE PLACE
Anywhere two people might want to resolve a problem.

THE SKETCH

[FIRST AND SECOND PERSON ENTER, STOP CENTRE AND SHAKE HANDS]

FIRST PERSON Thanks for coming.

SECOND PERSON I'm glad you rang because, frankly, I was going to ring you.

FIRST PERSON We can't go on like this, that's for sure.

SECOND PERSON No. My feelings exactly.

FIRST PERSON There must be a way to stop all this bickering. The church is splitting down the middle.

SECOND PERSON Everyone has strong feelings about it—it's obviously important.

FIRST PERSON Even the community is aware of the problem. It's...embarrassing. Non-believers are watching in amazement while Christians battle this thing out.

SECOND PERSON It's a shame. No argument there.

FIRST PERSON The people who should be showing the love of Jesus to the world are fighting each other. No wonder people have stopped coming to church.

SECOND PERSON I know, I know. It breaks my heart. Yet it *is* important.

FIRST PERSON Important, yes—but is it so important that the name of Christ should suffer because of our differences?

SECOND PERSON I agree with you in principle. If we can find a way to unite the church again, we should. But it won't happen until we resolve the question.

FIRST PERSON [SIGHS] Of course.

SECOND PERSON Well?

FIRST PERSON Well.

SECOND PERSON The future of the church is at stake. If

	we don't get this settled, we'll lose half of our people to start their own church.
FIRST PERSON	One half or the other... What a dilemma. People are willing to destroy the church and bring ridicule to the name of Christ...
SECOND PERSON	It's turned into a very passionate issue.
FIRST PERSON	Yes...
SECOND PERSON	So... what's your answer? Are we going to sing choruses in the morning worship or stay with traditional hymns?

[THEY FREEZE AS THE DISCUSSION LEADER ENTERS. IN TIME, THEY EXIT]

THE QUESTIONS

1. Read 1 Corinthians 1:10–17 and Philippians 2:1–4. What causes divisions in the church?

2. Are you currently experiencing divisions in *your* church? What is causing them? How is your church resolving such conflicts?

3. Under what circumstances are divisions acceptable within the church? What beliefs or doctrinal positions are so important as to divide churches? What conflicts are you currently seeing in the church that *shouldn't* be causing the divisions they're causing?

4. How can churches resolve the divisions within?

5. What is the apostle Paul's answer to divisions (see Philippians 2:5–11)?

THE VISITORS

THE TOPIC/THEME
Church visitors

THE SITUATION
Two visitors to a church hope to get noticed during the coffee-time after the service.

THE CHARACTERS
LAURA
GRAHAM
KATE

THE PLACE
A church hall.

THE SKETCH

[COFFEE-TIME AFTER A CHURCH SERVICE. GRAHAM AND LAURA ARE STANDING, COFFEE CUPS IN HAND, WATCHING THE PEOPLE AROUND THEM]

LAURA It was an enjoyable worship service.

GRAHAM Uh huh. I think this coffee time afterwards is a good idea. This is the first church we've visited who do it.

LAURA The reverend said it was a chance to meet visitors.

GRAHAM [PAUSE] Nobody seems very interested.

LAURA I'm sure they're busy just...uh...

GRAHAM Talking amongst themselves?

LAURA Well...yeah. Give them a minute to notice us.

[PAUSE]

GRAHAM They seemed quite warm and friendly in the service.

LAURA They did. I'm sure it's just a matter of time.

[PAUSE]

LAURA Maybe we're standing in the wrong place.

GRAHAM We're in the middle of the room.

[PAUSE]

GRAHAM Maybe we should go home now.

LAURA [SIGHS] I suppose we should. Unless we should take the initiative...try to talk to someone ourselves.

GRAHAM That's always so awkward.

LAURA We should try.

[KATE CROSSES, GRAHAM STEPS FORWARD TO INTERCEPT HER]

GRAHAM [CLEARING THROAT] Hello.

KATE [CAUGHT OFF-GUARD] Hello.

GRAHAM I'm Graham, this is my wife Laura.

KATE Oh, hello.

LAURA Hello.

GRAHAM We're visitors.

KATE Oh? How nice.

[PAUSE]

KATE This is your first time then?

GRAHAM Yes... we're visitors.

KATE [NOT SURE WHAT TO SAY] You live in the area?

GRAHAM Just moved in a few weeks ago. We've been church-shopping and thought we'd... you know.

KATE I'm glad you did. Welcome. It was nice meeting you.

[SHE SMILES AWKWARDLY, THEN EXITS. GRAHAM AND LAURA EXCHANGE SYMPATHETIC GLANCES, THEN MOVE TO EXIT IN THE OPPOSITE DIRECTION]

GRAHAM So, where do you want to go *next* Sunday?

[THEY EXIT]

THE QUESTIONS

1. Does this remind you of any church you've attended—your own church, for example? How would you feel if you were Laura and Graham?

2. Does your church have a system to ensure that newcomers are welcomed? If not, can you suggest one?

3. Kate made an effort to greet Laura and Graham, but it fell flat. What could Kate have done differently?

4. How much does 'feeling welcome' rely on Laura and Graham? What should *they* do to meet people?

PARTY INVITATION

THE TOPIC/THEME
Communication

THE SITUATION
A daughter is invited to a party and seeks her mother's advice about it.

THE CHARACTERS
MOTHER
SARAH

THE PLACE
A home.

THE SKETCH

[SARAH ENTERS FROM SCHOOL, DROPS HER BOOKS ON THE FLOOR NEXT TO THE CHAIR AND SITS DOWN. SHE TAKES OFF HER SHOES AS HER MOTHER—OBVIOUSLY RUNNING IN TEN DIRECTIONS AT THE SAME TIME—ENTERS. SHE IS CARRYING CLOTHES TO BE FOLDED AND PUT AWAY. SHE SITS AND HURRIEDLY BEGINS THE TASK]

MOTHER Hello, Sarah. You're home from school early. Don't leave your shoes in the middle of the floor.

SARAH [PULLS SHOES TOWARDS HER] Sorry.

MOTHER How was school?

SARAH Same as usual. Oh—I was invited to a party.

MOTHER [STOPS FOLDING CLOTHES] I don't have time to do this. Be a dear? I have a meeting at the church tonight. [STANDS, MOVES TO EXIT] A party? How nice. [EXITS]

SARAH Friday night.

MOTHER [ENTERING] Have you seen the stack of papers I left on the kitchen table?

SARAH No.

MOTHER I don't remember moving them. I hope your father didn't throw them away.

SARAH The only problem is that I told the minister I'd go with the youth to visit the nursing home. I can't decide what to do.

MOTHER [ENTERING, LOOKING AROUND] I need those papers for tonight. It wouldn't do for the chairperson of the committee to lose her papers.

SARAH There're going to be loads of people at that party. All the really popular ones. What do you think?

MOTHER Maybe I left them in my handbag. [EXITS AGAIN]

SARAH I could always go to the nursing home *next* week. I don't think anyone'll care.

MOTHER [ENTERS WITH HANDBAG AND PAPERS, RELIEVED] Here they are. [BEAT] Right. I'm off to my meeting. I'm glad you were invited to a party. I remember how important it was when I was in school. I'll be home around eight. Tell your father. Left-overs are in the 'fridge. [SHE EXITS]

SARAH [SHRUGS] I'll go to the party then.

[SHE EXITS]

THE QUESTIONS

1. What was the fundamental problem between the mother and daughter in this sketch? Is there anyone in your life that this reminds you of?

2. What is the outcome of a lack of communication between two people—particularly a mother and daughter?

3. Advise the mother in this sketch about her relationship with her daughter.

4. What should the daughter have done to get her mother's full attention to her question?

5. Taking time to *listen* has become a problem in many modern families. What can members of a family do to help increase communication?

FUN TO TALK TO

(Adapted with permission from CARE for the Family's *Family Matters*)

THE TOPIC/THEME

Compatibility

THE SITUATION

Two women talk about the 'long lunches' one has been taking with a male co-worker.

THE CHARACTERS

LINDA
ROSEMARY

THE PLACE

An office.

THE SKETCH

[AN OFFICE. ROSEMARY ENTERS WITH SOME WORK PAPERS AND SITS DOWN AT HER DESK. LINDA APPROACHES ROSEMARY'S DESK]

LINDA Ah—*there* you are. I've been looking for you. Long lunch, was it?

ROSEMARY I was just a little late getting back. Did I miss something?

LINDA No, I'm being nosey. You went to lunch with Paul today?

ROSEMARY Yes, I did. So?

LINDA So it's the third time in two weeks.

ROSEMARY I didn't know you were keeping count. Really, Linda, it's only a few lunches with a business associate.

LINDA [LOWERED VOICE] A 'business associate'? This is Paul Saunders we're talking about. He's very handsome, very intelligent, and very eligible. Are you telling me the two of you are only discussing 'business'?

ROSEMARY [SMILES] Well...he *is* a lot of fun to talk to. He seems to know about *everything*.

LINDA [KNOWINGLY] Hm. Does he know about Michael?

ROSEMARY He knows I'm married, if that's what you're saying. It's nothing to worry about, Linda.

LINDA [CAUTIONING] Rosemary...

ROSEMARY [DEFENSIVELY] I like being with him, that's all. He's...exciting. You know.

LINDA And Michael?

ROSEMARY I love Michael. It's just that he's...*Michael*.

THE QUESTIONS

1. What did Rosemary mean by that last statement? What does this tell you about Michael?

2. Is Rosemary wise to have lunches with Paul Saunders? What prediction would you make for the future of the relationship between Rosemary and Paul.

3. Can men and women be attracted to each other—become good friends—and *not* wind up physically involved? Why or why not?

4. Have you ever been—or are you currently—good friends with someone of the opposite sex apart from your mate? How does your mate feel about that?

5. If you were good friends with Michael and saw Rosemary at lunch with Paul, would you tell Michael? If so, what would you say? Considering Rosemary's last statement about Michael, what advice would you give to Michael?

THE FIGHT

(Adapted with permission from CARE for the Family's *Family Matters*)

THE TOPIC/THEME

Constructive arguing

THE SITUATION

A man comes home to his angry wife.

THE CHARACTERS

HUSBAND

WIFE (Kate)

THE PLACE

A home (a small table could be set up with dishes that Kate is drying and putting away).

THE SKETCH

[A HOME AT THE END OF THE WORK DAY. KATE IS IN THE KITCHEN, BANGING AROUND ANGRILY. THE HUSBAND ENTERS]

HUSBAND [APPROACHING, OFF-STAGE] Kate, I'm home. [ENTERING] Oh, there you are.
[NO RESPONSE, SHE SIMPLY BANGS THE POTS AND PANS AROUND]

HUSBAND Is something wrong?
[MORE BANGING AROUND]

HUSBAND Darling, will you stop demolishing the kitchen and tell me what's wrong?

WIFE You know perfectly well what's wrong!

HUSBAND No...I don't. Really I don't. Kate? Kate!
[MORE BANGING]

HUSBAND Kate, please. What's happened? Why are you so angry?

WIFE You don't know? You *really* haven't a clue?

HUSBAND No!

WIFE Typical. If you don't know, I'm certainly not going to tell you!

HUSBAND Look, Kate, I can't read your mind. Am I supposed to *guess*? Is that what you want?
[RENEWED BANGING AROUND]

HUSBAND Kate! What in the world do you want me to do?!?

WIFE Do whatever you like. I don't care.

HUSBAND This isn't fair! I hate it when you get like this.

WIFE *Hate* it, do you? Are we talking about *hate* now?

HUSBAND [BACK-TRACKING] No—not *hate*—but...[GROANS] I can't talk to you when you're in one of these moods.

WIFE Fine. Then don't talk to me at *all*.

[WITH A CRASH OF POTS AND PANS, SHE STORMS OFF STAGE. HUSBAND WATCHES HER GO THEN, EXASPERATED, FOLLOWS]

HUSBAND [PLEADING] Kate!

[HE EXITS. THE DISCUSSION LEADER ENTERS]

THE QUESTIONS

1. What was the fundamental problem with the couple in this sketch? Have you ever been in a similar argument with someone? What was the outcome?

2. Do you think Kate handled this argument well? Do you think the husband handled it properly? What could each have done differently?

3. If you're married, list three specific areas that cause the most difficulty in your relationship. How do you and your spouse resolve those conflicts?

4. When you argue, do you 'shut down' communication with the person you're arguing with? If so, why? If you argue, do you limit yourself to the specific reason for the argument or do you bring in other grievances?

5. What does the Bible say about resolving conflict?

WORRIED

THE TOPIC/THEME

Dating those who don't believe

THE SITUATION

A young woman shares the turmoil she has with her boyfriend.

THE CHARACTERS

CINDY
DENISE

THE PLACE

Anywhere two girls would feel comfortable talking.

THE SKETCH

[CINDY AND DENISE ENTER]

CINDY I've got a problem.

DENISE What's wrong?

CINDY Dave.

DENISE That bloke you've been seeing? I've had a look at him—what could possibly be wrong?

CINDY I don't think he's a Christian. In fact, I *know* he isn't a Christian.

DENISE That's a problem?

CINDY You know it is.

DENISE Yeah, I suppose. So... convert him.

CINDY It's not that easy. He... he doesn't like it.

DENISE What?

CINDY When I talk about my faith. Now I don't know what to do.

DENISE Meaning?

CINDY I think I'd better break up with him.

DENISE No...

CINDY What else can I do?

DENISE A little tolerance might go a long way.

CINDY It has nothing to do with tolerance. It has to do with *me*—what I believe. That's... that's important to me. My faith is... all that really matters. And I want it to matter to the one I share my life with.

DENISE But you don't have to *break up*, do you? That's so extreme. Can't you be patient and, you know, pray about it?

CINDY I don't have time to be patient. I'm afraid I'm going to make a terrible mistake.

DENISE Why would you do that?

CINDY Because I think I'm in love with him.

[THEY FREEZE FOR A MOMENT. THE DISCUSSION LEADER ENTERS. AFTER AN APPROPRIATE TIME, THEY EXIT]

THE QUESTIONS

1. Should Christians ever date those who aren't Christians? If so, under what conditions? If not, why not? What fundamental differences exist between Christians and those who aren't Christians? Are they important enough to prohibit romantic relationships?

2. Consider 2 Corinthians 6:14–18. How would you answer question 1 in the light of the apostle Paul's statements?

3. Considering her feelings, how would you counsel Cindy?

4. Have you ever dated or even loved someone who did not share your religion? What was the outcome of the relationship? What particular pressures did the difference in religion bring to your relationship?

EXPECTATIONS

THE TOPIC/THEME

The differences between men and women (expectations)

THE SITUATION

A man and woman go for a stroll during a party.

THE CHARACTERS

PETER (a friendly and confident party-goer)
LINDA (a rather anxious companion)
THERESA (Linda's sister)

THE PLACE

A park bench.

THE SKETCH

[PETER AND LINDA ENTER, STROLLING. THEY STOP AT THE PARK BENCH]

PETER [SITTING DOWN] Let's sit down. I'm getting tired.

LINDA [STANDING, NERVOUSLY] I'd better not. I should get back to the party.

PETER What's your hurry?

LINDA I should go back. My sister will be wondering where I am.

PETER Don't worry about her. With all that dancing, I'm sure she's not giving you a second thought.

LINDA Still—

PETER Come on...have a seat. Are you afraid of me?

LINDA No. Should I be?

PETER I'm as harmless as they come. Why are you so tense?

LINDA [SHE SITS ON THE EDGE OF THE BENCH, AS IF SHE MIGHT SPRING AWAY AT ANY MOMENT] Because I probably shouldn't be out here, that's why. I shouldn't have come to this party at all. [AS A STATEMENT] They're all the same, aren't they? Everybody drinks themselves to paralysis and smokes until the room is toxic and the guys are watching the girls and the girls are watching the guys and...I know how it'll turn out.

PETER How *what* will turn out?

LINDA The evening. It's too much for me. And this walk—I could've written it down before I left my house. Typical.

PETER What are you on about?

LINDA You asking me to come out here. The gallant knight rescuing the fair maiden from a boring party. You're nice. We talk awhile. But all along you're thinking we might do a little snogging. And, if you're charming enough, you might be right. Then, for you, it'll be an enjoyable party, a *successful* party. For me, it'll be the start of all the anxiety—wondering if you'll ring me tomorrow, wondering if I'll see you again, wondering how I'll feel when you *don't* call, wondering what to do or say if I go to another party and you're there and we'll have those awkward moments when you make a lot of excuses but I'll know you never *intended* to call, you just wanted someone to snog with and I'll feel cheap and you'll feel put-upon and one of us will have to leave early or endure a night of discomfort and, frankly, I don't think I can handle it, all right?

[PAUSE]

PETER Maybe I should go back to the party. [HE GETS UP AND EXITS THE WAY HE ENTERED]

[THERESA, LINDA'S SISTER, ENTERS]

THERESA Oh, there you are. Great party, huh?

LINDA It stinks. No one will talk to me. Can we go home now?

[SHE STANDS UP AND EXITS THE OPPOSITE DIRECTION FROM WHENCE SHE CAME. THERESA WATCHES HER, STUNNED]

THERESA Linda? [FOLLOWS HER] Linda! [EXIT]

THE QUESTIONS

1. What do you think of Linda's assessment of Peter's intentions for her—and the outcome she predicts? Is she right or wrong? Explain your answer.

2. What might Peter's expectations be? How do you think he felt about Linda's 'outburst'?

3. Linda complains that the party 'stinks' because no one will talk to her. What does this tell you about Linda's character?

4. Have you ever been in a situation like Linda's? How closely does her comments reflect your own experience? Have you ever been in Peter's position? If so, how did you feel and how would you have reacted to someone like Linda?

5. At the heart of this sketch is an observation about the differences between men, women and their respective expectations. Do you think this sketch is correct in its observation? Explain your answer.

MARTIN

THE TOPIC/THEME
Dysfunctional behaviour

THE SITUATION
A man needs a Reverend's help with his homelife.

THE CHARACTERS
MARTIN
REVEREND

THE PLACE
Reverend's office [or Vicarage].

THE SKETCH

[THE REVEREND ENTERS, SITS DOWN AT HIS DESK TO WORK. MARTIN ENTERS FROM THE OPPOSITE SIDE, SHEEPISHLY]

MARTIN Good morning, reverend. Can I have a word?

REVEREND Good morning, Martin. What can I do for you?

MARTIN It's my wife again, reverend.

REVEREND Oh? What now?

MARTIN Same old thing, reverend. Same old thing.

REVEREND *Which* same old thing? You two have several.

MARTIN It's along the flavour of physical violence to one's person, I'd say.

REVEREND *Whose* person?

MARTIN Perhaps mine.

REVEREND Did she hit you?

MARTIN Maybe.

REVEREND Did *you* hit *her*?

MARTIN Possibly.

REVEREND Did she throw you out?

MARTIN Could be.

REVEREND Were you at the pub again last night?

MARTIN You could say that.

REVEREND Martin, it's terribly early in the morning for this. Which was it?

MARTIN Maybe all of them.

REVEREND Explain.

MARTIN Well, you see, I was out drinking all night and I just know that when I go home that she'll hit me with something, then—providing I'm still conscious—I'll hit her back and then she'll throw me out.

REVEREND [PAUSE] Why do you do it, Martin?

MARTIN I can't help it, reverend, it just happens that way sometimes. You know how it is.

REVEREND No, I don't. We've talked about this again and again, Martin. I don't understand what you want me to do. This situation has become a tradition for you and your wife.

MARTIN [SHRUGS] My parents had the same traditions.

REVEREND Martin—

MARTIN But this is the last time, reverend. I swear on my Mother's eyes it is.

REVEREND Don't make your dead mother a party to your weaknesses.

MARTIN All I want you to do is go with me. Would you do that much? Just go with me. Then maybe she'll be reasonable. Would you do that just this once?

REVEREND Martin, I have a lot to get done today. I don't think—

MARTIN [DROPPING TO HIS KNEES, PLEADING] Oh, *please*, reverend. Please, I swear I'll never do it again. Please!

REVEREND For crying out loud, man. Get up! Have some dignity.

MARTIN Say you'll do it. I won't get off my knees unless you do.

REVEREND Don't tempt me, Martin. It could do wonders for your praying.

MARTIN Just this once, please?

REVEREND Well...

MARTIN Please?

REVEREND Just this once. *Only* this once.

MARTIN Thank God. My knees couldn't take it otherwise. [STANDS UP]

REVEREND Or your head.

MARTIN [FORCES A LAUGH] That's right, reverend. That's right.

REVEREND Tell me one thing: don't you and your wife get tired of living like this?

MARTIN Tired of it? [SHRUGS] I don't suppose we know any other way to live.

[THEY EXIT AS THE DISCUSSION LEADER ENTERS]

THE QUESTIONS

1. Assess the relationship between Martin and his wife. What's wrong with it?

2. How should the Reverend counsel Martin and his wife?

3. Martin seems to consider his relationship with his wife 'normal'? Is it? Explain your answer.

4. How do people—married or not—become used to certain types of 'questionable' behaviour in their lives?

5. Martin mentions that his relationship with his wife is similar to his parents' relationship? Do you think there's a connection? Is it possible to change behaviour we've learned from our parents?

THE QUESTION

THE TOPIC/THEME

Evangelism

THE SITUATION

A question about becoming a Christian triggers a curious response.

THE CHARACTERS

BOB

GEOFF

THE PLACE

Anywhere two people might feel comfortable to talk.

THE SKETCH

[BOB AND GEOFF ENTER TOGETHER]

BOB Thanks for meeting me, Geoff.

GEOFF No problem. What's up?

BOB It's a bit awkward, really. I've been curious.

GEOFF Curious?

BOB About this change in you. You know, bringing your Bible to work, talking about your faith—things like that.

GEOFF Yeah?

BOB So what's it all about?

GEOFF What do you mean?

BOB What's *really* going on? Why are you doing it?

GEOFF Because I believe in it.

BOB Right, but...how? I can't make sense of it. You've got this bloke named Jesus and He died and if I believe in Him, then I'll go to heaven.

GEOFF Something like that.

BOB But *why*? Why did He have to die?

GEOFF Because He was the Lamb of God whose blood had to be shed for the remission of our sins so that we could be redeemed according to the riches of His grace.

BOB Uh...yeah?

GEOFF Yeah! It's propitiation, isn't it? That way we could be justified to righteousness!

BOB Of course.

GEOFF So...does that answer your question?

BOB Yeah, it does.

GEOFF Good!

BOB I'll never understand it, not in a million years. I just needed you to confirm it for me.

[HE EXITS. GEOFF IS CONFUSED]

GEOFF [CALLING AFTER HIM, FOLLOWS] Bob? Maybe I didn't explain it right. Bob?

THE QUESTIONS

1. Did Geoff handle Bob's question effectively? Explain your answer.

2. What would you have done differently from Geoff?

3. In the simplest way possible, explain your understanding of how a person becomes a Christian.

THE QUERY

THE TOPIC/THEME
Evangelism

THE SITUATION
A question about becoming a Christian triggers a curious response.

THE CHARACTERS
BOB
DAN

THE PLACE
Anywhere two people might meet to talk.

THE SKETCH

[DAN AND BOB ENTER TOGETHER]

BOB Thanks for meeting me, Dan.

DAN My pleasure, Bob. What can I do for you?

BOB It's a bit awkward, really. I've been curious.

DAN Curious?

BOB About this change in you lately. You know, the way you're always smiling and talking about your faith—things like that.

DAN Yeah?

BOB So what's it all about? I'd like to know.

DAN [SINCERELY] Praise the Lord.

BOB Huh?

DAN I've been praying you would ask me.

BOB You have?

DAN Oh, yes! And just last Sunday Barbara Wilkins had a word of knowledge that you would ask me about my faith.

BOB Barbara... word... *what*?

DAN Barbara Wilkins at church. She knew you were going to do this.

BOB She said my name in church?

DAN Not you, literally, but someone like you. It was a vision, actually. Symbolic.

BOB Really?

DAN Yeah!

BOB So—what's it all mean?

DAN Oh, man, it's brilliant! God sends His Spirit inside of you and you raise your hands and just... just *praise* Him all the time!

BOB Praise Him? Why would I—er, I'm confused.

DAN That's all right. You're allowed to be confused. It's like speaking in tongues. You don't have to know, someone else'll interpret.

BOB Speaking in—

DAN Tongues, yeah. It's fantastic. You don't know until it happens to you. Praise the Lord!

BOB But what about Jesus?

DAN [SHRUGS] Oh—you have to believe in Him, too. [BRIGHTLY] And *then* you can ask to be filled with the Spirit! It's wonderful! I'm so glad you asked!

BOB Er, yeah...so am I.

DAN Well, do you want to do it?

BOB Do what?

DAN Pray!

BOB Pray?

DAN Yeah...so you can have what I have!

BOB Thanks, but...I think I'll wait until it makes a little more sense to me.

[HE EXITS. DAN WATCHES HIM GO, CONFUSED, CALLS AFTER HIM]

DAN [FOLLOWING] But it doesn't have to make sense! Bob?

[HE EXITS. THE DISCUSSION LEADER ENTERS]

THE QUESTIONS

1. Did Dan handle Bob's question effectively? Explain your answer.

2. What would you have done differently from Dan?

3. In the simplest way possible, explain your understanding of how a person becomes a Christian.

DIRTY LAUNDRY

THE TOPIC/THEME
False faces

THE SITUATION
Two girls react to an argument they've witnessed at a church social gathering.

THE CHARACTERS
JANET
DONNA

THE PLACE
A church gathering.

THE SKETCH

[AT THE DRINKS TABLE. JANET AND DONNA WALK ON TO GET THEMSELVES SOME PUNCH]

JANET How embarrassing.

DONNA What?

JANET Michael and Ginny. If I were her, I would've shrivelled up in the corner and died.

DONNA What? You mean their fight?

JANET What else? Good grief, do they have to do it in public—and at *church*?

DONNA [SHRUGS] We're all friends. It's not like they were on the nine o'clock news or anything.

JANET Friends or not, it's humiliating to see it.

DONNA Humiliating? I don't know about that. At least they kissed and made up. I'd rather see that than watch them fight now and hear about the divorce later. That's what *my* parents did.

JANET But why couldn't they fight at home? That's what *my* parents do.

DONNA Really? [SHRUGS] Maybe they didn't feel like waiting until they got home.

JANET I was raised not to air my dirty laundry in front of everyone. It's nobody's business. It's very...inappropriate.

DONNA Janet, maybe they felt so comfortable with us that they thought they could argue here. I don't mind. It's nice to see how a real marriage works rather than the 'perfect pretend' most of the adults play. This is church, right? I thought we're supposed to be ourselves here. [SHE WALKS AWAY]

JANET Yes, but...he's the *pastor*.

[JANET EXITS AS THE DISCUSSION LEADER ENTERS]

THE QUESTIONS

1. Would you say your church is a place where people of all backgrounds, with any type of trouble, on any level of difficulty could come, feel welcome, and find answers to their needs? Why or why not? If the answer is 'no', what should you—and your church—do about it?

2. Do you feel you can truly 'be yourself' at church? Why or why not? Do you ever find yourself playing a 'role' at church—Christian or otherwise—as you try to be what you think others expect you to be?

3. Are you aware of people who seem to behave one way at church and yet behave differently when they're at home or at school? If so, why do you think they act so differently? Do you act differently at church than you do anywhere else? Why or why not?

4. People are often on 'guard' in social situations—wearing false faces that hide what's really going on in their lives. How would you feel if someone you knew suddenly dropped the false front and let you see a few of his or her warts? How would you react to these scenarios:

   A friend you thought you knew well tells you in the confidence of a prayer request that he/she is 'struggling with homosexuality'.

   Your youth pastor announces that he and his wife are having marriage difficulties and may separate for a while.

   You find out from a close Christian friend that he or she never reads the Bible, prays and, if the truth be known, has serious doubts that Christianity is even worthwhile.

A girl you know to be a role-model as a Christian leader confesses that she's pregnant.

Someone admits to you that he or she once took drugs regularly and is suffering the temptation to go back to regular use again.

5. The Bible says in James 5:16, 'Therefore, confess your sins to one another, and pray for one another so that you may be healed...' In the sketch, Janet says it's 'inappropriate' to air 'dirty laundry' in public. What is the difference, if any, between confessing one's sins and 'airing dirty laundry'?

GRANDAD

THE TOPIC/THEME
Family

THE SITUATION
A grandfather gives his opinion about families (among other things).

THE CHARACTERS
GRANDAD

THE PLACE
Anywhere.

THE SKETCH

[GRANDAD ENTERS]

GRANDAD

I used to be a young man. Honest. I've got the pictures to prove it. They look a bit funny now—the pictures, that is—because I look so...so young. My hair was a solid colour and my own two legs were enough to get me around. Funny. When you're young, you can't imagine being old. When you're old, you can't imagine how you got there so fast. I have no explanation or insights for this. That's simply the way it is. Fact is, I have few explanations or insights for anything. Being old and being wise don't always go hand-in-hand. I'm a little disappointed about that. The only thing I've really learned is that I've got a lot left to learn—and less time to learn it.

What did I come up here to talk about? Oh, yes. Families. I don't understand what all the fuss is about families these days. Seems like everybody's talking about them. There are all kinds of books and—what do you call those things?—video machines. Videotapes with lectures about how to be a family. I suppose they're all right. I tried to watch one but fell asleep during the part about things women want men to know about husbands but were afraid to ask—or something like that. I get it confused. Maggie—that's my wife—she says people spend so much time listening and watching that they never have time to do what they're supposed to.

I hate to admit it but she can be downright intelligent for a senile old woman.

It's her birthday today. I can't tell you how old she is. She kept telling me to forget about it and finally I did...completely. All I know is that she was born sometime in the twentieth century...I think. When was the Panama Canal built? I think her birth had something to do with that!

Maybe I'll make her a cake. Last year I put a candle on for every year I thought she was alive and had to ring an ambulance after she tried to blow them out! That's when we were on our holiday in Florida. Englewood. It's got a beach. My sister Nancy and her husband Jack get all kinds of peculiar-looking seashells there. They make—what do you call them?—nick-knacks out of them. They gave me one for my birthday that looks like Winston Churchill. Clever what they do with those things.

I went to the beach with them one day and had the seagulls eating out of my hand. You hold up a piece of bread and they fly up and sort of hang there in mid-air and eat. I hate seagulls. They're rats with wings. I just feed them so they'll get close enough for me to hit them with my cane. It really surprises them. I had to quit, though. Did you know they actually have a fine for clobbering seagulls? It's ridiculous. Only in America.

I got sidetracked, didn't I? What was I talking about?

[REMEMBERS] Oh yes, I was going to tell you about our grandchildren. God love them. They like to climb all over me. It hurts sometimes but I don't mind. I think God's calling in this life was for me to be a grandfather. I really do. And since I couldn't be one as a young man, I think, then, that that's the biggest blessing of being old.

I don't know what the fuss is about—being a family. You simply are. It's not always easy but, then again, nothing worth having comes easily. Ask Maggie. She gave birth to two of the best family I ever knew.

And that's all I wanted to say, actually.

[HE EXITS AS THE DISCUSSION LEADER ENTERS]

THE QUESTIONS

1. Do you agree or disagree with Grandad's assessment that there are too many 'helps' for the family and not enough action? Explain your answer.

2. Grandad states that he doesn't understand all the fuss about being a family—'you simply are'. Do you agree or disagree? How is being a family now different from when someone Grandad's age was starting one? Why does it seem harder to keep families together now?

3. Grandad expresses disappointment that being old doesn't necessarily go hand-in-hand with being wise. Do you know any older people who are wise? Do you ever seek their counsel? How do you think society treats old people these days?

4. Grandad mentions the joy he has of being a grandfather. Have you ever thought about being a grandparent? What do you think you'll be like? Describe yourself as you might be in ten years?—twenty years?—thirty years?—fifty years? Would you like to be treated then the way you treat older people now?

FOR THE GOOD OF THE FAMILY

(Adapted with permission from CARE for the Family's *Family Matters*)

THE TOPIC/THEME
Family Priorities

THE SITUATION
A husband comes home late from work and wants to say goodnight to the children.

THE CHARACTERS
PETER
RACHEL

THE PLACE
Peter's and Rachel's home.

THE SKETCH

[RACHEL AT THE KITCHEN TABLE DRINKING SOME TEA AFTER AN EXHAUSTING DAY. PETER PEEKS IN, ENTERS]

PETER Hello, darling. I'll just go up and say goodnight to the kids—

RACHEL No you don't. I've just settled them. Give me a hand with the dishes.

PETER But they can't be asleep yet...I'll just give them a quick goodnight kiss.

RACHEL No, Peter! I've been the last hour getting them settled down. If you go up now, they'll never get off to sleep. It's not fair.

PETER Fair! I've come racing back from a meeting and I can't say goodnight to my own children?

RACHEL Racing, were you? You said you'd be home by six thirty! Nicky wanted to show you his history report. I thought we were having supper together tonight.

PETER The group from the head office came in. I phoned you, Rachel.

RACHEL At quarter past six.

PETER I thought I'd be home before this.

RACHEL You always say that. Look, Peter, it's up to you. If you want to spend time with the children— or me—you're going to have to get home earlier. That's all.

PETER Oh, marvellous! I'll just sacrifice my career, is that the idea?

RACHEL No...

PETER I'm not doing it for *me*, you know. Whatever I do is for the good of the family.

[THEY FREEZE IN POSITION AS THE DISCUSSION LEADER ENTERS. THEN THEY EXIT]

THE QUESTIONS

1. Consider Rachel's point of view in this sketch. Do you think she is being reasonable in what she feels—and says to Peter? Why or why not?

2. Consider Peter's point of view. Is he being reasonable in his response? Why or why not?

3. Peter equates his work with 'the good of the family'. Is he right to believe this? What about time with the family? If you had to choose between spending more time at work or more time with your family, which would you choose?

4. Whether they realise it or not, both Peter and Rachel are discussing *priorities* in their lives. Think about your life then list the three things that are most important to you. If you're married, compare this list with your spouse's.

5. Now list the three things you spend most of your time on—the first being the highest amount of time, etc. How does this list compare with the list you created from question 4?

DAD'S HOTLINE

THE TOPIC/THEME

Fatherhood

THE SITUATION

We eavesdrop on four conversations on a crisis hotline for fathers.

THE CHARACTERS

FATHER-TO-BE

CRISIS HOTLINE OPERATOR

THE PLACE

This might be most effective pre-recorded on audio-tape and played to your audience. If that isn't possible, the stage could be set up with tables and phones at opposite ends. The operator enters and sits at one of the tables. Soon thereafter, our father-to-be enters in a slight panic, grabs phone and dials. The phone rings or the operator sees the light on the board, punches the button, and picks up the receiver.

NOTES:

Rather than play these scenes back-to-back, it is suggested that you perform them intermittently throughout your discussion time.

THE SKETCH

CRISIS HOTLINE I

[WE'RE EAVESDROPPING ON A CRISIS HOTLINE FOR FATHERS. A VERY NERVOUS AND PANICKED FATHER-TO-BE NEEDS HELP...PHONE RINGS...CLICK AS IT'S ANSWERED AT THE HOTLINE]

CRISIS HOTLINE Hello—DADS Helpline.

FATHER-TO-BE Is this the crisis hotline?

CRISIS HOTLINE Hotline for fathers, yes.

FATHER-TO-BE Oh. Well, what if I'm not a father yet?

CRISIS HOTLINE Yet?

FATHER-TO-BE My wife. She just told me she's pregnant.

CRISIS HOTLINE Congratulations!

FATHER-TO-BE Congratulations! Are you kidding? I'm not ready for this. I...I don't want to be a father.

CRISIS HOTLINE You don't? Is this your first?

FATHER-TO-BE Of course it is! You think I'd react like this if it wasn't?

CRISIS HOTLINE Yes.

FATHER-TO-BE I mean, it's not like I *don't* want to be a father, you know? I'm all for it in principle. But...I mean, it's all so sudden. I don't...I mean...I don't know how I'm going to *cope*. We're going to have a *baby*, for crying out loud!

CRISIS HOTLINE That's the traditional way to become a father...yes.

FATHER-TO-BE That's fine for *other* people, but not me. I have no idea...that is, I don't know how to change nappies. And what if it cries in the middle of the night? And how will I know if the milk is too hot? And what if it won't stop crying and its head explodes or...or...it piddles all over my best suit or...it looks like my Uncle Stan or...I won't know what to do!

CRISIS HOTLINE	Sir?
FATHER-TO-BE	And what about everything I'm going to give up! Huh? I don't think I'm ready for the change...the sacrifice...it's too much to expect for me to just up and—
CRISIS HOTLINE	Sir?
FATHER-TO-BE	I'm not very...Uh, yeah?
CRISIS HOTLINE	How long has your wife been pregnant?
FATHER-TO-BE	Two hours! She just told me this afternoon.
CRISIS HOTLINE	What I mean is—
FATHER-TO-BE	Oh—the doctor thinks she's about two-and-a-half months.
CRISIS HOTLINE	So you have over six months to prepare yourself for the baby's arrival?
FATHER-TO-BE	Oh?
CRISIS HOTLINE	Your wife told you she's pregnant today, but that doesn't mean the baby will come tomorrow. You have time.
FATHER-TO-BE	Oh...yeah. Time.
CRISIS HOTLINE	So...relax. Why don't you take your wife out for a meal—to celebrate?
FATHER-TO-BE	Uh...good idea. Yeah. That would be nice.
CRISIS HOTLINE	Because in seven months, you won't be able to.
FATHER-TO-BE	*What?!?*

[DIAL TONE—OR ACTORS FREEZE IN POSITION AS THE DISCUSSION LEADER ENTERS]

THE QUESTIONS

1. Have the members of your group who *aren't* fathers describe what they imagine fatherhood to be like.
2. Have the members of your group who *are* fathers describe what fatherhood *is* like.
3. Compare the answers to the first two questions.

CRISIS HOTLINE II

[A FEW MONTHS LATER. SAME CHARACTERS AS BEFORE. PHONE IS RINGING ON THE LINE. CLICKS AS IT IS ANSWERED AT THE HOTLINE]

CRISIS HOTLINE DADS Helpline.

FATHER-TO-BE Hi—yeah—I talked to you guys a few months ago.

CRISIS HOTLINE You did?

FATHER-TO-BE My wife is pregnant. She's going to have a baby.

CRISIS HOTLINE One usually means the other!

FATHER-TO-BE Yeah, right. I...I'm just confused, you see. I don't know if, you know, things are normal.

CRISIS HOTLINE Is your wife seeing a doctor?

FATHER-TO-BE Yeah. But I'm not talking about her. I'm talking about *me*. We've been taking these classes and I'm not sure I'm getting it right. The breathing, you know?

CRISIS HOTLINE What aren't you sure about?

FATHER-TO-BE If I'm breathing right! See, I've been practising in front of a mirror—just to make sure I've got it—but then I start to see these little spots and get all dizzy and—

CRISIS HOTLINE Excuse me, sir, but *you're* not supposed to do the breathing.

FATHER-TO-BE I'm not?

CRISIS HOTLINE No. Your *wife* needs to breathe properly. Your job is simply to coach her.

FATHER-TO-BE [PAUSE] Ah!

CRISIS HOTLINE Didn't they explain that to you in the class?

FATHER-TO-BE They might have but...I passed out at one point and maybe missed it!

CRISIS HOTLINE You passed out?

FATHER-TO-BE	Yeah—when they explained about what happens in the delivery room. I get squeamish watching my wife pluck her eyebrows—I don't know how I'm going to survive this.
CRISIS HOTLINE	I'm sure you'll be fine.
FATHER-TO-BE	Do you really think so?
CRISIS HOTLINE	Yes... what you're experiencing is normal.
FATHER-TO-BE	Oh, good. That's a relief. [PAUSE] Is it also normal for me to crave chocolate-covered brussels sprouts with just a hint of french dressing and grapefruit juice?

[DIAL TONE—OR THE ACTORS FREEZE IN POSITION AS THE DISCUSSION LEADER ENTERS]

THE QUESTIONS

4. Ask the fathers and mothers in your group to explain how they coped with the imminent arrival of their first child.

5. Did they go to birth-preparation classes? If so, have them describe what they were like and some aspects of how they needed to prepare.

CRISIS HOTLINE III

[SAME AS BEFORE—MONTHS LATER]

CRISIS HOTLINE — DADS Helpline.

FATHER-TO-BE — Hi. I think I have a problem here. A *major* problem. But I don't want to over-react. My wife says I've been over-reacting to this whole pregnancy.

CRISIS HOTLINE — Oh? What's the problem this time?

FATHER-TO-BE — My wife is in labour.

CRISIS HOTLINE — Really?

FATHER-TO-BE — Yes. I was in the middle of converting my lovely oak-panelled study into a cheesy-looking blue and yellow nursery when she told me she was in labour.

CRISIS HOTLINE — Maybe this is bad advice but...shouldn't you get her to the hospital?

FATHER-TO-BE — [PAUSE] Do you think so? I don't want to over-react.

CRISIS HOTLINE — I think you're okay on this. That's standard procedure. Take her to the hospital.

FATHER-TO-BE — Okay. I believe you. Do you think I have time to clean the paint brushes first?

CRISIS HOTLINE — That depends on your wife. Where is she now?

FATHER-TO-BE — Oh!—uh—hang on. [OFF PHONE] Honey? Honey, where did you...Oh. [ON PHONE] She's out in the car. Boy, she doesn't miss a trick.

CRISIS HOTLINE — So she's all right for now.

FATHER-TO-BE — I think so. She's in the back seat with her legs in the air.

CRISIS HOTLINE — [BEAT] Don't take time to clean the brushes. Take her to the hospital.

FATHER-TO-BE — Well...okay...if you think so. Should I start my breathing now?

CRISIS HOTLINE Go ahead. But get moving. Carefully but quickly.

FATHER-TO-BE [BREATHING HEAVILY] Okay. Thanks.

[DIAL TONE—THEY FREEZE IN POSITION AS THE DISCUSSION LEADER ENTERS]

THE QUESTIONS

6. Ask the parents in your group to recall their labour experiences.

CRISIS HOTLINE IV

[SAME AS BEFORE—EXCEPT OUR FATHER-TO-BE IS IN THE AFTERGLOW OF HAVING JUST BECOME A FATHER]

CRISIS HOTLINE	DADS Helpline.
FATHER-TO-BE	Hey! Hey!
CRISIS HOTLINE	DADS Helpline.
FATHER-TO-BE	It's me! It happened! I'm a father! You should've seen it! It was...it was a *miracle*!
CRISIS HOTLINE	Well, congratulations!
FATHER-TO-BE	Oh, she's beautiful. She's incredible. And...and she's *mine*. *My* little girl.
CRISIS HOTLINE	I'm very happy for you.
FATHER-TO-BE	She looks a little like Jabba-The-Hut—but the doctor says that's normal. Oh, I wish you could see her.
CRISIS HOTLINE	Send us a picture.
FATHER-TO-BE	I will, I will—you guys have been very helpful.
CRISIS HOTLINE	That's what we're here for.
FATHER-TO-BE	Yeah, thanks. Oh, man! This is unbelievable...Incredible. In a million years I couldn't tell you what this feels like.
CRISIS HOTLINE	Treasure it.
FATHER-TO-BE	Yeah, I will...[PAUSE] So...what am I supposed to do next?
CRISIS HOTLINE	What?
FATHER-TO-BE	She's born now. Should I start looking for colleges? What?
CRISIS HOTLINE	One step at a time, I think.
FATHER-TO-BE	Right...Sure...Like what?
CRISIS HOTLINE	Have you called anyone?
FATHER-TO-BE	I called you.
CRISIS HOTLINE	Your family? Her family?
FATHER-TO-BE	[PAUSE] Oh...Yeah...Good idea.
CRISIS HOTLINE	All the best, then.
FATHER-TO-BE	Right. Thanks. [PAUSE] This is the best

	thing that's ever happened to me, you know.
CRISIS HOTLINE	It gets better.
FATHER-TO-BE	That doesn't seem possible.
CRISIS HOTLINE	It is, man. It is.

[DIAL TONE—THEY FREEZE IN POSITION AS THE DISCUSSION LEADER ENTERS]

THE QUESTIONS

7. Ask the parents in your group to talk about the problems and conflicts they've experienced as parents.

8. Ask the parents in your group to talk about the pleasures they've enjoyed as parents.

DEPRAVED

THE TOPIC/THEME
The generation gap

THE SITUATION
A preacher talks about the depravity of this generation.

THE CHARACTERS
SPEAKER (Should be an adult)

THE SKETCH

[COULD BE ANYWHERE. THE SPEAKER ENTERS, THEN ADDRESSES THE AUDIENCE WITH GREAT PULPIT-POUNDING FERVOUR]

SPEAKER

The times change so quickly, don't they? No sooner were we finished with the war than society went into a... a moral upheaval. Young people behaved in ways not to be believed—or tolerated. The music they listened to... the lack of modesty in their clothes... it was all so scandalous. How did they expect me, a man of God, to react? They were part of my flock and, like any good shepherd, I had to lead them, even if it meant keeping them from the cliff-edge by striking them with my staff. [ASIDE] (I'm speaking metaphorically, of course.) [RESUMING] I was determined to meet their wayward rebellion with equal energy and force. Sunday after Sunday I preached and railed and presented a vigorous attack against the sins that seemed to become more acceptable. Sunday after Sunday the attendance decreased to just a handful—the older, more faithful few—and the young people simply stopped coming. I suppose they loved the world too much. It was a sign of the times, really. I don't suppose the youth of our country were ever more in danger of being swallowed up by depravity than they were in that year of... 1927.

[SPEAKER EXITS AS THE DISCUSSION LEADER ENTERS]

THE QUESTIONS

1. It has been said that every generation believes its youth are more decadent than previous generations. Do you think that's true or not? Explain your answer. In what ways might our generation be in greater moral danger than generations past? What can be done about it?

2. Compare the preacher's description of the youth of 1927 with today's youth. Why do you think the young people stopped going to his church? What could/should the preacher have done to keep the young people coming to church? Compare your answer with programmes in your own church to reach out to the young.

3. How can a church alienate its young people by trying *too hard* to reach out to young people?

4. To attract young people, how much should a church change in the following areas:

   Sermons (content, etc.)
   Style of music in the worship services (The use of contemporary musical styles with worshipful lyrics, etc.)
   Social activities

   How would you like to see your own church change in these areas? What about the older members who enjoy more traditional approaches? Should they concede their desires for the younger members or should the younger members concede to the older? Can a church satisfy both generations? If so, how?

5. Consider the apostle Paul's advice to young Timothy in 1 Timothy 4:12; 5:1–2; and 2 Timothy 2:22. How would you apply these verses to your own life—and the young Christians of this generation?

ROB'S WILL

THE TOPIC/THEME
God's will in dating

THE SITUATION
A young man believes he knows God's will about the girl who has just broken up with him.

THE CHARACTERS
JONATHAN
ROB

THE PLACE
Anywhere two people would feel comfortable talking privately.

THE SKETCH

[JONATHAN AND ROB ARE SITTING, TALKING. JONATHAN IS TRYING TO BE SYMPATHETIC TO ROB'S SITUATION]

JONATHAN So Emily broke up with you. How depressing.

ROB [SHRUGS] Not really.

JONATHAN What do you mean? You're not upset?

ROB No. Not at all.

JONATHAN But...I thought you *loved* Emily.

ROB I do.

JONATHAN And you're not heart-broken because she broke up with you?

ROB No. It's a minor set-back.

JONATHAN I don't get it.

ROB I have confidence in something greater than what Emily *thinks* she wants.

JONATHAN Oh? And what might that be?

ROB God.

JONATHAN God?

ROB God. You see, I believe it's His will that Emily and I should be together.

JONATHAN [SCEPTICALLY] God's will.

ROB Uh huh! I prayed about it and I believe it. She's the one God wants for me.

JONATHAN By any chance, did God reveal this to Emily as well?

ROB Not yet. I might tell her today—providing she's spiritually mature enough for God's will to reach her.

JONATHAN So you're not bothered that she's going out with Richard tonight.

ROB Not at all. Not even Richard—popular as he is—can thwart God's will.

JONATHAN You're sure about this?

ROB Absolutely. Richard can't thwart God's will.

JONATHAN I mean about Emily being the one God has picked for you.

ROB By faith, I claim it.

JONATHAN But, Rob—

ROB If God can number the hairs on my head, then He must know who I should spend the rest of my life with.

JONATHAN Emily.

ROB Correct.

JONATHAN But... what if you're wrong?

ROB God wouldn't let me feel like this and be wrong at the same time. 'Get thee behind me, Satan.'

JONATHAN [SHRUGS] Suit yourself.

ROB I think I'll walk over to her house—tell her the good news. Pray for me, will you?

JONATHAN Oh... uh, sure!

ROB Thanks.

[HE GETS UP TO EXIT, GIVES JONATHAN THE 'THUMBS UP'. JONATHAN RETURNS THE SALUTE. ROB EXITS. JONATHAN SHRUGS, ADDRESSING EVERYONE AND NO ONE]

JONATHAN But *who* should I pray for?

[HE EXITS. THE DISCUSSION LEADER ENTERS]

THE QUESTIONS

1. Do you think Rob is correct in his thinking about God's will? Should Emily get back together with Rob based on 'God's will'? Explain your answer. How would you feel if you were Emily?

2. Have you ever made a decision based on your understanding of God's will—only to have it proved otherwise? How did you feel?

3. How can anyone understand God's will? (How does God communicate with us?)

4. Make a list of the ways God reveals His will to man—according to examples from the Bible.

TRAPPED

(Adapted with permission of CARE for the Family's *Family Matters*)

THE TOPIC/THEME
Home life

THE SITUATION
A man explains the state of his home life to a friend.

THE CHARACTERS
PAUL
BOB

THE PLACE
A pub.

THE SKETCH

[PAUL IS AT A TABLE HAVING A DRINK, BOB ENTERS, JOINS HIM. BOTH ARE DRESSED AS IF THEY'VE JUST FINISHED A DAY AT THE OFFICE]

PAUL You look terrible. I knew the meetings were long, but I didn't think they were *that* long.

BOB It wasn't the meetings. I'm shattered...

PAUL Cheer up, mate. It's the end of the day and you have a whole weekend to look forward to.

BOB [NOT ENCOURAGED] Yeah...the weekend.

PAUL Come on! Two days off to relax with the family. Better than slaving at the office.

BOB You don't know my family.

PAUL Oh? Is it so bad?

BOB Well...the minute I get home, my wife has a complete list of jobs for me to do around the house. That generally takes me up to Sunday night. I have a son in the throes of teenage rebellion who couldn't say a civil word to me if his life depended on it—and it sometimes does—and a daughter who locks herself in her room with a television, stereo and hair dryer that she has on all at the same time.

PAUL Sounds like a nice place to go home to...

BOB Home? It's not a home. It's a *trap*.

[THEY FREEZE IN POSITION AS THE DISCUSSION LEADER ENTERS. AFTER A MOMENT, THEY EXIT]

THE QUESTIONS

1. Can you sympathise with Bob? How?

2. If you had to pick a word or phrase to describe your home life, what would it be?

3. What counsel would you give Bob to get rid of his feelings of being 'trapped'? How can Bob improve his life at home?

LIFE OF THE PARTY

(Adapted with permission from CARE for the Family's *Family Matters*)

THE TOPIC/THEME

Humour

THE SITUATION

Two girls discuss another girl's use of humour at a party.

THE CHARACTERS

RHONDA

ALISON

THE PLACE

A drinks table at a party.

THE SKETCH

[RHONDA ENTERS, FIXES HERSELF A DRINK AT THE DRINKS TABLE. ALISON ENTERS TO DO THE SAME]

RHONDA Hello, Alison. What do you think of the party?

ALISON It's okay, I suppose.

RHONDA You don't like it?

ALISON Nah, the party's good. It's just some of the people.

RHONDA Who?

ALISON I was over watching Jennifer. You know, 'Miss Life of the Party'. I don't know why they think she's so funny.

RHONDA What? I think she's hysterical.

ALISON She's rude. Did you hear the way she was picking on poor Scott? He's the butt of most of her jokes. I can't figure out why he dates her.

RHONDA Maybe he thinks she's funny, too.

ALISON Why? She jokes about how he dresses, how bad he does at school...and this time she even made remarks about his kissing. In front of *everyone*. She's rude. I'm not used to people who talk like that—especially a Christian.

RHONDA That's just the way she is. It's harmless. Everyone knows she's only doing it for a laugh.

ALISON Sure. Anything for a laugh. Sarcasm, criticism, dirty jokes...just so it's funny.

RHONDA Aren't you being a little hard on her?

ALISON I don't think so...I was thinking about talking to her but I'm afraid I'll become one of the punchlines.

RHONDA Don't be so stuffy. If you knew her better, you'd understand.

[RHONDA EXITS]

ALISON Why should I have to understand?

[SHE EXITS THE OPPOSITE DIRECTION. THE GROUP LEADER ENTERS]

THE QUESTIONS

1. What kind of person is Jennifer? What kind of person is Alison? What kind of person is Rhonda? Who do you side with?

2. Alison makes some fairly hard statements about Jennifer and her sense of humour. Would you agree or disagree with her conclusions? How would you answer Alison's last question?

3. Rhonda seems more tolerant of Jennifer and considers Alison 'stuffy'. Do you agree or disagree with Rhonda's attitude? Explain your answer.

4. Sometimes people are far more tolerant of certain things—and even certain people—if it (or they) makes them laugh. For example, references to sex are often accepted if they're done through innuendo and have a humorous result. Critical attacks on a person are often disguised through sarcastic (yet funny) jabs—to give two examples. How much should Christians tolerate in the name of humour? Are all forms of humour acceptable to the Christian? If not, which types of humour (or jokes) would you exclude? By what criteria do you draw such distinctions?

5. Apply Ephesians 5:3–4; 19–20; Colossians 4:6; and Matthew 12:33–37; 15:10 and 17–20 to this discussion.

SPONTANEOUS

THE TOPIC/THEME
Keeping the spark alive in relationships

THE SITUATION
A couple lament the lack of spontaneity in their relationship.

THE CHARACTERS
RICHARD
ALISON

THE PLACE
A home.

THE SKETCH

[A HOME. A QUIET EVENING]

RICHARD [SIGHS] What's happened to us, Alison?

ALISON Sorry?

RICHARD When did we get so... so domestic?

ALISON What are you on about, Richard? *Who's* so domestic?

RICHARD Look at us! You're doing the Times crossword puzzle and I'm reading a magazine article about lagging the pipes. What's happened to us? Where's the youthful fire—the reckless romance—the spontaneous passion?

ALISON Oh! That's the answer to seven across.

RICHARD [CONFUSED] What?

ALISON Seven across. Instant, unplanned. [WRITING] Spontaneous.

RICHARD Alison! Put the crossword away. We're too young to act so old. Let's be mad... impulsive ... wild!

ALISON You're serious.

RICHARD Of course I am! Why don't we go upstairs and... make it an early night? What do you say?

ALISON [DOUBTFUL] I don't know...

RICHARD Why? What's wrong?

ALISON It's not Friday!

[THEY FREEZE IN POSITION AS THE DISCUSSION LEADER ENTERS. AFTER A MOMENT, THEY EXIT]

THE QUESTIONS

1. What can couples do to keep the spark of interest and excitement alive in relationships?

2. List five things couples can do spontaneously simply to change their routine.

3. Do you know any couples who have settled into a set routine and seem to lack any spontaneity? What is their relationship like? Do you admire their relationship or would you suggest ways of improvement?

4. Apply the same questions from Number 3 to couples who seem *very* spontaneous.

LATE AGAIN

THE TOPIC/THEME
Relationships: (lateness)

THE SITUATION
A husband has to deal with his wife's constant tardiness.

THE CHARACTERS
HUSBAND
WIFE

THE PLACE
A bedroom at home.

THE SKETCH

[WIFE IS AT A TABLE, MAKING UP HER FACE FOR AN EVENING OUT. THE HUSBAND ENTERS. HE IS AGITATED]

HUSBAND There you are! I've been waiting in the car. Come on! We're going to be late.

WIFE [PUTTING ON MAKEUP] I'm coming.

HUSBAND That's what you said ten minutes ago. Will you please hurry?

WIFE I'm hurrying! [BEAT] Oh—look. I've smudged my lipstick.

HUSBAND Fix it in the car!

WIFE It's too dark in the car. It'll only take a—

HUSBAND Elaine, we're *late*—again—as usual. Why do we have to go through this?

WIFE You tell me! I'm doing the best I can.

HUSBAND Can't you go faster? You knew what time we had to be there.

WIFE You want me to look nice, don't you?

HUSBAND Yes, but I'd like to be on time just for once. Why do we always have to fight about it?

WIFE I don't know. I want to look nice and you want to be on time. Which is more important?

HUSBAND [GROWLS] I don't know why we have to choose.

WIFE Oh no!...this colour is the wrong shade!

HUSBAND Elaine!

[THEY FREEZE IN POSITION AS THE DISCUSSION LEADER ENTERS. THEN THEY EXIT]

THE QUESTIONS

1. Is this scene familiar to you? How? What is the fundamental problem with this couple?

2. If you were the husband in this sketch, how would you feel about the wife's constant lateness? Do you know someone who is always late for things? How do you feel when you're kept waiting for him or her? What reason(s) does this person often give for being late?

3. If you were the wife in this sketch, how would you feel about the husband's anger and frustration?

4. Are either character's feelings justified? Explain your answer? Are *you* often late for engagements? Why? How do you think people feel about your being late? List ways you could work to be on time.

5. What can these two characters do to reconcile their conflict? What practical advice would you give them to solve this problem?

6. It has been said that being late shows a lack of respect for other people. Do you agree or disagree? Why or why not? How do you think it reflects on a Christian's witness to others to be late all the time?

DESIRE

THE TOPIC/THEME
Lust

THE SITUATION
John is trying to help Bob with his problem.

THE CHARACTERS
JOHN
BOB

THE PLACE
Anywhere two men would feel comfortable talking about personal problems.

THE SKETCH

[JOHN IS SITTING, WATCHING BOB. BOB IS AGITATED, PACING]

JOHN Of course I'll pray with you, but do you realise what you're asking?

BOB What else am I supposed to do? You don't know what it's like.

JOHN That's not true.

BOB You're married, John. How could you possibly understand? I'm 28 years old and single. *Very* single. I don't have a girlfriend—or even a *prospective* girlfriend. I...I feel lonely sometimes.

JOHN That's normal.

BOB Normal, yes. Natural. But not spiritual. I think about things. I fantasise. I...I do things I shouldn't do. Oh, it's never the biggies—you know, fornication or adultery, but [POINTS TO HEAD] it's all up here. So I want God to take it all away. I'd rather have no sexual feelings at all than to go on with this torture.

JOHN But God gave those sexual feelings to you. Do you realise what you're asking Him to do? What if He honours your prayer?

BOB Then I can get on with other areas of my life.

JOHN What if you meet someone and decide to get married?

BOB Then I'll pray to get the feelings back.

JOHN Come on, Bob, it's not as if God can simply flip switches on and off inside of you.

BOB Why not? I'm desperate, don't you see? I want to be pure. I want to live in a way that's pleasing to God—but how can I when my mind and my desires are out to get me?

JOHN There must be another way.

BOB Yeah? Like what?

JOHN We'll pray for discipline.

BOB Discipline! I'd have to be Mr Spock to have that kind of discipline. It's all pent up inside me, John. This...appetite, this energy. What am I supposed to do?

JOHN [PAUSE] I don't know.

BOB Right. So let's pray that God will take the desires away from me. What else can I do?

[THEY FREEZE IN PLACE. DISCUSSION LEADER ENTERS. THE ACTORS EXIT AFTER A MOMENT]

THE QUESTIONS

1. Define lust. Where does it come from? What is its result? What does the Bible say about lust? (See Matthew 5:28; 1 John 2:16–17 and Romans 13:14.)

2. Bob is sincere in his desire to be pure, but is equally vexed over his inability to control his thought-life. What would you suggest that he do?

3. Have you ever struggled with this problem? If so, what have you done about it? If not—share your secret with the rest of us!

4. Would you say that lust is particular to men or do women suffer from it as well? What are the differences, if any, between a woman's lust and a man's lust.

5. Consider the apostle Paul's words in Romans 7:15–24. What was his answer (chapter 8)? List five practical methods for dealing with lust.

CHRISTMAS AT HOME?

(Adapted with permission from CARE for the Family's *Family Matters*)

THE TOPIC/THEME

Marriage: dealing with your spouse's relatives

THE SITUATION

A husband and wife argue over plans for Christmas.

THE CHARACTERS

HUSBAND
WIFE

THE PLACE

A home.

THE SKETCH

[WIFE ENTERS, HUSBAND FOLLOWS—THEY ARE IN THE MIDDLE OF AN ARGUMENT]

HUSBAND Now, darling, be reasonable.

WIFE I am! You're the one who's going back on his word.

HUSBAND I'm not! I never promised we would go to your mother's for Christmas this year! I *couldn't* have. I would have choked on the words before they came out!

WIFE What do you think we're going to do? Spend Christmas with *your* family?

HUSBAND It's not such a bad idea. At least *my* family *likes you.*

WIFE My mother likes you! Really!

HUSBAND Ha! Do you think I've already forgotten what she said last Christmas? When you wanted to kiss me under the mistletoe? Do you?

WIFE Not that again.

HUSBAND She said: 'why don't you hang *him* and kiss the mistletoe!' That's what she said. The woman hates me. I'm not spending another Christmas with someone who hates me. It tends to spoil the mood.

WIFE At least my mother knows how to celebrate Christmas. All your family do is eat cold turkey and watch the same TV programmes on different sets!

HUSBAND [PAUSE] So?

WIFE So what?

HUSBAND So why do we have to go to either? Why can't we stay home this year? Just you and me? We'll celebrate Christmas in our own special way—start a few of our own traditions. Who knows? We may never want to spend Christmas with our relatives again!

WIFE [PAUSE, SCRUTINISES HIM] You're kidding, right?

HUSBAND [PAUSE, THINKING ABOUT IT] Yeah. They'd never let us get away with it.

WIFE [AS SHE EXITS] Then we're going to my mother's.

HUSBAND [FOLLOWING HER OFF] We're *not* going to your mother's!

[THEY EXIT. THE DISCUSSION LEADER STEPS FORWARD]

THE QUESTIONS

1. Have you and your spouse ever argued over where to spend Christmas? How did you resolve your argument? How would you advise this husband and wife to resolve this argument?

2. How much pressure do you think in-laws (and family) put on couples to spend time with them during holidays? Is this pressure reasonable? How can a husband and wife—particularly newlyweds—balance the need to start their own family holiday traditions and still fulfil family obligations?

3. Do you have any general rules you apply to making decisions about how much time to spend with family—not only during holidays, but at other times of the year?

PRE-MARITAL QUESTIONS

THE TOPIC/THEME
Marriage preparation

THE SITUATION
While saying goodnight, an engaged couple recall their evening together.

THE CHARACTERS
PHILIP
MELISSA

THE PLACE
A front door.

THE SKETCH

[PHILIP AND MELISSA ENTER AS IF APPROACHING THE FRONT DOOR TO MELISSA'S HOUSE]

PHILIP Thank you, Melissa. You're all right, you know.

MELISSA I am? Why?

PHILIP These pre-marriage classes. They were your idea, as I recall.

MELISSA Oh yeah...

PHILIP I enjoyed it tonight. I think it's very important that we talk about the things we've been talking about. I only wish we'd done it sooner.

MELISSA Me, too. [BEAT] What do you mean?

PHILIP Well, seeing as how we're getting married in two weeks—I just think it might've been better not to, you know, take them so close to the actual event.

MELISSA Why?—Are you afraid you'll change your mind?

PHILIP No! Of course not! We're not going to learn anything about each other that'll change my mind. Not at this point, that is. I mean, we've been seeing each other for a long time. I like to think I know you pretty well.

MELISSA Same here.

PHILIP I think it's something we can tell our kids about. You know, the importance of pre—

MELISSA Hold on. Did you say 'kids'?

PHILIP Yes. Kids. Our children?

MELISSA But...I don't want to have any children.

PHILIP What?

[THEY FREEZE IN POSITION AS THE DISCUSSION LEADER ENTERS. SOON AFTER, THEY EXIT]

THE QUESTIONS

1. How well do you think you know your future spouse? If you think you know him or her well, offer opinions about the following subjects the way you think he or she would:

   - ☐ Religion: will you go to church together? Which church?
   - ☐ Finances: who will control your money?
   - ☐ Children: will you have any? If so, how many?
   - ☐ Holidays: where do you like to spend your holidays?
   - ☐ Family: how often would you like to see your family?
   - ☐ Sex: how often do you expect to make love in a week? do you feel comfortable talking about sexual problems?
   - ☐ Priorities: what's the most important thing to you?
   - ☐ Communication: can you tell your spouse-to-be the worst thing you've ever done?
   - ☐ Goals: what is the foremost goal in your relationship?
   - ☐ Job: if you have to choose between giving up your job or your spouse giving up his or hers, which would you choose?

2. Are you currently getting pre-marital counselling? Why or why not?

DEPRESSED

(Adapted with permission from CARE for the Family's *Family Matters*)

THE TOPIC/THEME
Mental illness

THE SITUATION
A conversation between a husband and wife about how good their lives are.

THE CHARACTERS
KYLE
CHARLOTTE

THE PLACE
The kitchen table in Kyle and Charlotte's home.

THE SKETCH

[A HOME. CHARLOTTE IS SITTING AT THE TABLE DRINKING A CUP OF TEA. SHE IS IN HER BATHROBE AND LOOKS DOWNHEARTED. KYLE ENTERS, DRESSED TO GO OUT FOR THE EVENING]

KYLE Charlotte? What are you doing? Do you know what time it is? We're going to be late.

CHARLOTTE I wanted a cup of tea.

KYLE But we're supposed to be there at seven.

CHARLOTTE I know.

KYLE Charlotte...

CHARLOTTE We have a good life—don't we, Kyle?

KYLE A good...? Yes, I suppose so.

CHARLOTTE We have a strong relationship, you and me. Wonderful kids. Friends. Good jobs. A nice home.

KYLE We have all those things, yes, but...?

CHARLOTTE I was just thinking, that's all. There's a lot to be thankful for.

KYLE You're right. [BEAT] Are you going to dress, then?

CHARLOTTE In a minute. I'll dress in a minute.

KYLE [MOVES TO EXIT] Don't be long.

CHARLOTTE Kyle?

KYLE Yes, love?

CHARLOTTE If our life is so good... [BEGINS TO CRY] Why am I so unhappy?

KYLE Oh, Charlotte...

[HE MOVES TO HER AND HOLDS HER CLOSE. THEY FREEZE AS THE DISCUSSION LEADER ENTERS. WHEN APPROPRIATE, THEY EXIT]

THE QUESTIONS

1. What is Charlotte's problem? Have you ever had times when you felt unhappy for no apparent reason? How did you pull yourself out of it? Have you ever felt as though you simply cannot cope with the many demands in your life?

2. Define depression. What causes it? Do you know anyone who has ever suffered from depression? If so, how did they behave? Ultimately, what did they do about it? Have you ever suffered from depression for a long period? If so, how did you respond? Did you get counselling?

3. How is depression different from bad moods, 'off' days or periods of melancholy?

4. Though the Bible assures us of God's constant love and care and asks us to rejoice at all times, can Christians become depressed? If so, what should they do about it? How can you, as a brother or sister in Christ, help those who suffer from depression?

GOOD OLD HARRY

THE TOPIC/THEME
Mid-life crisis

THE SITUATION
Two men watch a friend's behaviour at their local.

THE CHARACTERS
MATTHEW
DONALD

THE PLACE
A pub.

THE SKETCH

[A PUB—WHERE EVERYONE IS DRINKING PINTS OF LEMONADE, NATURALLY! DONALD ENTERS AND SIGNALS TO THE BARMAN FOR ANOTHER DRINK. MATTHEW ENTERS FROM THE OPPOSITE SIDE AND JOINS DONALD]

MATTHEW Hello, Donald. Everything all right?

DONALD Yeah, just thought I'd wet the old whistle before going home.

MATTHEW Did you see...? [GESTURES OFF STAGE]

DONALD Harry? [SMILES] Yeah.

MATTHEW Look at him...over there with that girl. What's her name?

DONALD I haven't the foggiest.

MATTHEW He changes them every week.

DONALD Half his age, she is.

MATTHEW Most of them are. What a change, eh?

DONALD What do you think did it...the toupee?

MATTHEW I don't know. He started wearing those wild shirts so you could see the hair on his chest.

DONALD He thinks it's sexy.

MATTHEW I wonder if *she* does.

DONALD How could a girl that age know? It must be the money he throws around. I don't know where he gets it.

MATTHEW Neither do I. I heard that Elizabeth took him for everything she could get in the divorce.

DONALD No surprise...the way he left her. Hell hath no fury...and all that.

MATTHEW I wonder what started it all?

DONALD I don't know. But I hope it doesn't happen to me.

MATTHEW I'll drink to that.

[PAUSE/BEAT]

DONALD Look at him...

MATTHEW [SHAKING HIS HEAD] Poor Harry.

[THEY FREEZE IN POSITION AS THE DISCUSSION LEADER ENTERS. AFTER A MOMENT, THEY EXIT]

THE QUESTIONS

1. Is Harry's problem familiar to you? How? Do you know anyone in their 30's or 40's who has suddenly changed his/her behaviour for no apparent reason? How did he/ she change?

2. What causes mid-life crisis? What are the symptoms? Is there any way to stop it?

3. How can Christians use the spiritual aspect of their lives to counter the effects of mid-life change?

4. What advice would you give to Harry if you had the chance? What advice would you give to Donald and Matthew to help Harry?

OVERDRAFT

(Adapted with permission of CARE for the Family's *Family Matters*)

THE TOPIC/THEME
Money

THE SITUATION
A husband and wife discuss their financial difficulties.

THE CHARACTERS
PHILIP
PAULINE

THE PLACE
A home [living room].

THE SKETCH

[PHILIP IS FINISHING UP A PHONE CONVERSATION. HE IS ANGRY, BUT TRYING TO REMAIN CORDIAL. PAULINE ENTERS TO CATCH THE END OF IT]

PHILIP [ON THE PHONE] Yeah...uh huh. Thanks for calling. [HANGS UP THE PHONE WITH A GROWL] Cow!

PAULINE That was a strange phone conversation. Who was it?

PHILIP The Bank Manager. She's got a nerve.

PAULINE What did she want this time?

PHILIP Said she's concerned about our overdraft. Concerned, my foot! Nosy more like. Has to squeeze every pound out of you. I'll bet she used to be one of those Olympic wrestlers!

PAULINE [CONCERNED] Philip—what about our overdraft?

PHILIP She said 'it's getting too high'. What business is it of hers, eh? It's not as if *she's* personally responsible for the money.

PAULINE Is it too high, Philip?

PHILIP No worse than anyone else's, love. It's the economy. High interest rates and all that. She had the gall to suggest that we're living beyond our means! Can you believe it?

PAULINE Are we?

PHILIP What kind of question is that? Prices keep going up and our salaries stay the same? What do they expect?

PAULINE But...I don't like high overdrafts, Philip. I don't like being in debt.

PHILIP Well, get used to it, love. There's *nothing* I can do about it.

[THEY FREEZE IN POSITION AS THE DISCUSSION LEADER ENTERS. AFTER AN APPROPRIATE INTERVAL, THEY EXIT]

THE QUESTIONS

1. Who controls the money in your family? When financial decisions are being made, who ultimately makes the final decision?

2. The concern of the bank manager and the reference to their overdraft might indicate that the couple in this sketch really *are* living above their means. How do you think couples get into that predicament?

3. How do you manage your finances? Do you have a long-term financial plan? How do you prioritise the use of your money?

4. What does the Bible say about money and its uses? (Read Ecclesiastes 5:10; 1 Timothy 3:3; 6:10; Matthew 25:14–30; Luke 17:7–10 and Hebrews 13:5).

5. What does the Bible say about indebtedness? (Read Psalm 37:21 and Proverbs 22:26–27).

A PLACE FOR EVERYTHING

THE TOPIC/THEME

Neatness

THE SITUATION

A daughter is going crazy trying to find where her mother puts things.

THE CHARACTERS

AMY

MOTHER

THE SKETCH

[AMY'S BEDROOM. SHE IS LOOKING AROUND FOR SOMETHING. FINALLY, SHE CALLS OUT]

AMY [TO HERSELF] I wonder where—[CALLING] Mum? Mum!

MOTHER [ENTERING] Yes, dear?

AMY Have you seen my shoes?

MOTHER Which pair?

AMY The black ones...with the strap. I had them out...next to the bed.

MOTHER They're probably in the wardrobe—where they belong.

AMY But I just took them off.

MOTHER An hour ago.

AMY Did their parking meter expire? Mum, couldn't you leave them alone?

MOTHER Amy, you know I can't stand clutter around the house.

AMY But they weren't cluttering the house. They were sitting innocently next to my bed where I knew they would be when I needed them. They weren't in your way.

MOTHER They're just as handy in the wardrobe as they were next to your bed. I don't know why it's such a trauma for you.

AMY It's a trauma because I can never find anything. I was almost late for school this morning because you moved my books.

MOTHER [AS SHE LEAVES] Well, your shoes are safe and sound in the wardrobe, all right? There's no sense getting upset about it.

AMY All right! All right! [SHE TURNS TO THE CHAIR, REACHING FOR SOMETHING, THEN CRIES OUT AGAIN] Mum—where is my sweater?

[SHE EXITS. THE DISCUSSION LEADER ENTERS]

THE QUESTIONS

1. If we were to define 'compulsive' as meaning 'fanatic' or 'obsessive', answer these questions: Are your parents compulsively neat, reasonable, or compulsively cluttered? Now answer that question for *you*. How does their behaviour in this area align with your behaviour? If there is conflict, how can you reconcile it?

2. Considering your answer to the previous question, what expectations would you have of your children in your own house?

3. What do you think compulsive neatness or compulsive messiness says about a person's character? Do you have any friends or acquaintances who are one or the other? How do you feel when you're visiting them? Does this neatness or messiness show up in other areas of their lives? Answer these same questions about yourself.

4. A Christian author once noted that the condition of his car was often a good indication of his spiritual state. If his car was cluttered and dirty, then it was more than likely he wasn't very disciplined about prayer and Bible study. If his car was clean and tidy, then he was usually in tune with his relationship with God. Respond to this thought in the light of the previous question.

5. What should Amy do about her mother? What do you think Amy will be like when she has a home of her own? Explain your answer.

IT WASN'T MY FAULT

THE TOPIC/THEME
Obedience

THE SITUATION
A young boy gives a defence for his behaviour.

THE CHARACTERS
ANDY (or Amanda)

THE PLACE
Andy's room.

THE SKETCH

[ANDY (OR AMANDA) ENTERS, SITS DOWN RESTLESSLY, STANDS UP AGAIN, THEN LOOKS AT AUDIENCE AS IF THEY'RE A PERSON WHO HAPPENS TO BE SITTING IN THE ROOM]

ANDY It's not fair, you know. Being sent to my room for something that wasn't my fault. Look at me. Don't you think I'm too old to be sent to my room? Six I am. Almost seven. And Mum sent me to my room. For what? Nothing. I didn't do anything wrong. All I was doing was knocking my ball around.

I couldn't help it if it went into Mrs Woodshin's back garden. She hates it when my ball goes into her back garden because I have to climb her fence to get it and her flowers always get in my way. She likes her flowers. I do, too, except when they get in my way. Mum said never to go in Mrs Woodshin's back garden but my ball was right in the middle of it, next to one of those gnome-thingies.

So I went to get my ball. It wasn't my fault. I didn't think she was home. I went to get my ball and was going to leave but Sashay came running up to me. Sashay is Mrs Woodshin's poodle. I don't like poodles. They're sissy-dogs. All they ever do is yap and go to the loo.

So I started bouncing my ball. That's all. It wasn't my fault that Mrs Woodshin's poodle kept getting under it. It was an accident. I bounced my ball and it hit Sashay. It made a funny noise. I would go: [MAKES BALL-BOUNCING NOISE]. And Sashay would go: [MAKES A NOISE LIKE A LOUD YAP FROM A

POODLE BEING HIT WITH A BALL]. So it sounded like: [PUTS THE TWO SOUNDS TOGETHER]. It sounded like the noises they make on the Flintstones. I thought it was funny.

Mrs Woodshin came out and didn't think it was funny at all. She said: [AS A VERY OLD WOMAN] 'You! You there! Stop bouncing that ball on my dog!' So I stopped. It wasn't my fault.

Then Sashay went to the loo all over the flowers. Sissy-dog. So Mrs Woodshin said [IMITATION MRS WOODSHIN AGAIN] 'Now my flowers are going to die!'

And then Mr Woodshin came out. My daddy says he's...he's...sea-nailed. Mr Woodshin yelled [IMITATING A VERY OLD MAN] 'You! You there!'

[NORMAL VOICE] Why do old people always yell that?

[MR WOODSHIN'S VOICE] 'What's the pest done now, Beatrice?'

And Mrs Woodshin said, [AS MRS WOODSHIN] 'This little new-sance made Sashay go to the loo on the flowers.

And he said: [AS MR WOODSHIN] 'Make him get the hose and wash them off.'

So I did. It wasn't my fault. Really. I was thinking about the *Wizard of Oz* when they threw water on the witch and she melted. That's all. And then I thought that Mrs Woodshin looked a lot like the witch. That's all. It wasn't my fault. The hose slipped. [PAUSE] She didn't melt. Mr Woodshin grabbed my ear and shook it and shook it [HE SHAKES HIS HEAD BACK AND FORTH TO ILLUSTRATE] so I tried to make him melt, too. He didn't. So they made me go inside and called my Mum.

She doesn't like me very much right now.

But it wasn't my fault. Maybe just a little. Probably a lot. My Daddy will give me a spanking when he gets home but he'll think it's funny. He thinks I'm funny a lot. But he still spanks me. I don't think that's funny at all.

Mum says she doesn't understand me. Dad says it's the sin nature. Mum says I'm of the devil. Either way, it wasn't my fault.

MOTHER [FROM OFFSTAGE] Come down here, Andy/ Amanda! Your father's home!

ANDY No, it wasn't my fault at all.

[HE SLOWLY TODDLES OFF]

THE QUESTIONS

1. What is the 'sin nature' the child's father referred to? According to the Bible, where does the 'sin nature' begin and how does it manifest itself in us? (See Genesis chapter 3 and Romans 5:12)

2. It has been said that children are living examples of the fall of man—in their blatant, seemingly unlearned knack for disobedience. Do you agree or disagree with that assessment?

3. Do you think people are basically good or basically evil? Defend your answer.

WOMEN

THE TOPIC/THEME

Ordination of women

THE SITUATION

A Vicar (Reverend) makes plans before leaving for a church meeting.

THE CHARACTERS

REVEREND
ASSISTANT

THE PLACE

A church office.

THE SKETCH

[A REVEREND IS GOING OVER CHURCH DETAILS WITH HIS ASSISTANT]

REVEREND Before I leave for the conference, I want to make sure we have all the programmes at the church covered for next week.

ASSISTANT Right.

REVEREND Did you ask John to co-ordinate the new house groups?

ASSISTANT Yeah, but he said 'No', so Emily Woodward is going to do it.

REVEREND And what about the Sunday school teachers for next week? Do we have those taken care of?

ASSISTANT Susan McBride said to leave it to her. She said Donna Milner and Nicola Roberts would lend a hand.

REVEREND Wonderful. You confirmed Nicholas for the Scripture reading?

ASSISTANT Nicholas is away.

REVEREND Then who will do it?

ASSISTANT Carol Owen said she would if we ever needed her.

REVEREND All right.

ASSISTANT I sorted out the food and refreshments for the youth night on Friday. Mary Donovan is going to get the ladies group to handle it.

REVEREND Excellent.

ASSISTANT Lynn Kerridge has pulled together some volunteers to get the weeding and pruning done on the church grounds on Saturday.

REVEREND I thought the men's group said they'd take care of that?

ASSISTANT They did—but they're going on a day-long fishing excursion and we need to have it done in time for the outdoor family parade the next day.

REVEREND Right. We have to get someone to set up chairs for that.

ASSISTANT Belinda Smith has it all sorted out.

REVEREND Brilliant! Well, then, I suppose I can leave for the conference with some peace of mind. It's good to know everything is under control.

ASSISTANT What *is* this conference by the way?

REVEREND Our association of churches wants to debate women's role in the Church. Apparently there are a number of women who are raising a fuss about taking on more responsibility in the services. I don't understand it. Why can't they accept scripture for what it says and forget about it? [AS HE EXITS] I can't imagine what they're thinking—taking part in the services. [EXITS]

ASSISTANT [THOUGHTFULLY] Hm. I can't imagine when they'd find the time. [EXITS]

THE QUESTIONS

1. What do you think of the ordination of women? Be specific. What is your church's position? Why do they hold such a position? Do you agree or disagree? Explain your answer.

2. Do you think the questions surrounding the ordination of women are biblical or cultural? Interpret the following Bible verses: 1 Timothy 2:11–12; 1 Corinthians 14:35 and Acts 2:17–18.

3. Is there any way to reconcile the opposing factions over the issue of the ordination of women? If so, how?

4. Do you know any ordained women? What do they feel about their positions? Does it cause them any problems? If so, what kind?

BE REASONABLE

(Adapted with permission from CARE for the Family's *Family Matters*)

THE TOPIC/THEME

Parental control

THE SITUATION

A young girl is headed out for the evening and her Mum wants to 'discuss' it.

THE CHARACTERS

AMY (teen)
MOTHER

THE PLACE

A home.

THE SKETCH

[THE MUM ENTERS WITH A BASKET OF CLOTHES TO BE FOLDED. SHE SITS AND BEGINS THE PROCESS. AMY ENTERS, CROSSES THE STAGE ON HER WAY OUT]

AMY See you later, Mum!

MOTHER Hold it! Where are you going?

AMY To Debbie's. You know. I told you.

MOTHER When—in my sleep? Which Debbie?

AMY Debbie Craig.

MOTHER [WITH OBVIOUS DISLIKE] Oh—her.

AMY [EXASPERATED] Don't start, Mum.

MOTHER What is it—another party? You know how I feel about her parties.

AMY No, Mum. We're going to a concert and then I'm spending the night at her house. Don't you remember?

MOTHER Spending the night? I think we need to talk about this.

AMY [GROANS] Mum, you already said I could go. I made the plans and everything.

MOTHER I don't remember Debbie Craig being involved. I only want to know more about it. Is that so terrible...a mother concerned about her daughter's welfare?

AMY It's a *concert*. That's all. And you won't know who the band is even if I tell you.

MOTHER I've been hearing a lot of bad things on the news about concerts. Drugs, wild behaviour...

AMY [EXASPERATED] *Mum!*

MOTHER Don't take that tone with me, Amy.

AMY [GETTING UPSET] Mum, I have to go. They're waiting for me!

MOTHER Amy, I think we need to sit down and talk about this situation—calmly and rationally.

AMY No, Mum! Every time we *talk* about something

it means you'll try to *talk* me out of it! That's how you always make me do what you want. Well, I don't want to talk about it—I'm leaving!

[SHE EXITS]

MOTHER Come back here, Amy! You're being very immature about this! [CALLING] Amy!

[SHE FOLLOWS AMY OFF AS DISCUSSION LEADER ENTERS]

THE QUESTIONS

1. The Bible says explicitly that children are to obey their parents (Ephesians 6:1–3; Exodus 20:12). Under what conditions may a child disobey a parent, if ever? Have you ever felt your parents were being unreasonable and you wanted to disobey them? Recount such an incident and its outcome.

2. In Ephesians 6:4; Paul cautions fathers not to provoke children to anger. How should you interpret this verse? How do you apply this verse in practical terms (specific to you and your parents)?

3. Amy complains that by discussing a problem her mother is really just manipulating her to do her mother's bidding. Does that seem to be true of the mother in this sketch? Do you ever feel your parents discuss (using discussion as a tool) things with you merely to persuade you to do what they want? if so, how do you react?

4. Someone once noted that 'rules without relationship result in rebellion.' How would you assess the relationship between this mother and daughter? Is your relationship with either of your parents similar to this? If so, how? if not, would you say that your parents are generally reasonable in their demands on you? What would you change if you could?

MODEST LIVING

THE TOPIC/THEME
Priorities

THE SITUATION
Over tea, Emily and Katie discuss family sacrifices.

THE CHARACTERS
EMILY
KATIE

THE PLACE
Katie's home. A tea table.

THE SKETCH

[EMILY AND KATIE ARE HAVING TEA TOGETHER]

EMILY It's nice to have a few minutes to ourselves. I don't get to see you much anymore.

KATIE You know where *I* am. You're the one who's always busy.

EMILY I know, I know. The house looks lovely, Katie.

KATIE Thank you.

EMILY Oh, I envy you—I really do. You have such a...modest lifestyle.

KATIE Modest? I'm not sure how to take that.

EMILY I mean it as a compliment. Your lifestyle is so...so simple. You have a nice place to live, all the things you really need...and you get to stay home with the children.

KATIE We have a modest lifestyle *because* I stay home with the children. We can't afford anything anymore—not the kind of things you and Nigel are able to buy.

EMILY That's exactly what I mean. We don't *need* most of the things we buy.

KATIE But they're wonderful to have, aren't they?

EMILY I'm not so sure. Sometimes it feels like we're on a treadmill. We buy more and more and we both have to work harder to maintain standards. I'd rather be home with the kids.

KATIE Would you? I thought you liked working.

EMILY It's all right—but the children are growing up so fast. I'm afraid I'm missing it.

KATIE What can you do...quit?

EMILY I could, but that would mean giving up some of the things we have...things we like to do.

KATIE I suppose that's part of it. If you want one, you'll have to forget about the other.

EMILY Honestly, I'm not sure it's a sacrifice we're ready to make.

[THEY FREEZE IN POSITION AS THE DISCUSSION LEADER ENTERS. AT AN APPROPRIATE TIME, THEY LEAVE]

THE QUESTIONS

1. React to Emily's attitude. Do you think her attitude is good or bad? Emily is obviously in the dilemma of affording a lifestyle versus time with the children. Do you think she is right or wrong in the choice she has made? Explain your answer.

2. If Emily's children had a say in their parents' choice, what do you think they'd want—a comfortable lifestyle or more time with their parents? Explain your answer.

3. Have you ever had to give up one thing you enjoyed for something or someone? Explain the circumstances behind your decision. How did you reach that decision? What was the outcome and how do you feel about it now?

4. Are people these days too obsessed with possessions? How does our society suffer as a result of materialism? What does the Bible say about possessions? (See Matthew 6:19–34 and apply Jesus' words to modern living and priorities.)

FOR THE KIDS

THE TOPIC/THEME
Reconciliation

THE SITUATION
Two friends discuss why the parents of one reconciled their marriage.

THE CHARACTERS
JEFF
ANDY
(Note: With minor alterations, this could be played by any combination of genders)

THE PLACE
A porch.

THE SKETCH

[ANDY HAS BEEN DOING SOME GARDENING AND HAS JUST SAT DOWN TO DRINK SOME SQUASH. HE WIPES HIS BROW WITH A RAG AND JEFF, HIS FRIEND, ENTERS]

JEFF Finished your gardening yet?

ANDY Almost. I have some trimming to do in the back corner. Hold your horses, the snooker club's not going anywhere.

JEFF I see your dad's car is back in the driveway.

ANDY Yep. He came back last night.

JEFF Uh huh. How long do you give them this time?

ANDY I'm not making any bets. He's acting different.

JEFF What do you mean?

ANDY He didn't give us all the usual apologies and promises and 'please forgive me' speeches. He and mum said they talked about it and would get help. They want to work the problems out.

JEFF That's something new. Do you believe it?

ANDY Yeah—I'd like to. He said a funny thing.

JEFF What?

ANDY He said they decided to work it out because of us kids. He said if it was up to them, they wouldn't try. But they'll do it for our sakes... us kids.

JEFF Wow! That *is* funny. Was he serious?

ANDY Yeah. I think so.

JEFF They're doing it for the kids. Pretty old-fashioned.

ANDY Yeah, I guess. But, you know... I'm not sure I'm comfortable with the idea... I mean, having someone do that much for me.

[THEY FREEZE IN POSITION AS THE DISCUSSION LEADER ENTERS. THEN THEY EXIT]

THE QUESTIONS

1. What do you think Andy means by 'I'm not sure I'm comfortable with the idea... I mean, having someone do that much for me'? Why wouldn't he be comfortable? How would you feel if two people made a life-changing decision based on your needs?

2. One might get the sense that Andy's parents were sacrificing their own desires for the sake of their kids. Do you think they were right or wrong to do this? Explain your answer. Have you ever given up something you wanted—or wanted to do—in order to do what was right, or help another person? What were the circumstances behind the decision and why did you decide to do it that way?

3. Read 1 Corinthians 6:1–10 and 8:1–13. There, the apostle Paul instructs the church of Corinth on two separate matters where individual 'rights' and 'desires' conflict with someone else's 'rights' and 'desires'. What does Paul advise us to do? How would you apply these verses to these situations:

    Christians around you believe dancing is wrong for Christians to do. Yet, you've been invited to a wedding reception where there will be dancing. Should you go? If you do, should you dance?

    Your brother (or sister) is a new Christian and thinks the rock music you like to listen to is spiritually unhealthy. What do you do?

    You like to wear many of the latest fashions—tops and bottoms that show off your physique. You think they look good on you. But someone of the opposite sex tells you such clothes are inappropriate for a Christian because it causes some to lust. How do you react?

    You love films but your girlfriend/boyfriend thinks they're a hindrance to yours (and her/his) Christianity. Do you continue to go to cinemas?

THE DATE

THE TOPIC/THEME
Relationships: Divorce

THE SITUATION
We see the conclusion of a date between a man and woman.

THE CHARACTERS
DANIEL
CHERYL

THE PLACE
The front door of Cheryl's home or flat.

THE SKETCH

[DANIEL AND CHERYL ENTER. THEY STOP CENTRE, AS IF THEY'VE APPROACHED CHERYL'S FRONT DOOR. DANIEL IS GENUINELY CONTENT. CHERYL IS VERY NERVOUS]

DANIEL This is it.

CHERYL Yes... it is.

DANIEL A quiet restaurant... good food... soft music... it was nice, wasn't it?

CHERYL Yes... very... thank you.

DANIEL Thank *you*. [AWKWARDLY] I don't want to be forward, Cheryl, but... frankly, I think you're unbelievable. I'm being sincere. The way you handled that rat-bag during the divorce, staying on top of your job, raising little Jennifer by yourself. You're remarkable.

CHERYL Thank you, Dan.

DANIEL I don't know how you've managed.

CHERYL [SHYLY] I've wondered myself.

DANIEL However you did it, I salute you. And I'm glad you went out with me tonight. It's one of the most enjoyable evenings I've had in a long time.

CHERYL Yes... it has been.

[PAUSE]

DANIEL Cheryl?

CHERYL Yes?

DANIEL May I... kiss you goodnight?

CHERYL [PAUSE, NERVOUS, UPSET] No, Dan... I'm sorry. I have to go in. Thank you for a wonderful evening.

[CHERYL TURNS AND EXITS. DAN WATCHES HER GO]

DANIEL [BEWILDERED, TO HIMSELF] What was that all

about? You'd think the woman had never been on a date before.

[HE SHRUGS AND EXITS IN THE WAY HE CAME. THE DISCUSSION LEADER ENTERS]

THE QUESTIONS

1. Cheryl obviously had an enjoyable evening with Dan, yet she ran away from him at the end of the date. What do you think Cheryl's problem was?

2. Through Dan's praise of Cheryl, we understand that she is divorced. What kinds of pressures are divorced people under in today's society?

3. Within a Christian context, what do you think of divorce? What are your feelings about people who are divorced? How should you as a Christian respond to the needs of divorced people? What do you think the church should do to help divorced people?

4. If there are any divorced people in your group, ask them if they would be willing to talk about their experience. Have any of them been in a similar situation to Cheryl? How did they feel? How did they handle the situation? How do divorced people cope with dating again?

THE PHONE

(Adapted with permission from CARE for the Family's *Family Matters*)

THE TOPIC/THEME
Relationships: Fathers

THE SITUATION
As a mother and son try to get a father's attention, a telephone call brings him to life.

THE CHARACTERS
MOTHER
FATHER
JAMES (their son)

THE PLACE
A tea table at home.

THE SKETCH

[A HOME. FATHER IS AT THE TABLE READING THE PAPER WHILE THE MOTHER IS FINISHING DINNER PREPARATIONS. JAMES, THEIR TEENAGE SON, IS IN THE OTHER ROOM WATCHING TELEVISION. MOST OF THESE LINES SHOULD OVERLAP]

MOTHER [CALLING] James, your dinner's on the table!
JAMES [FROM THE OTHER ROOM] OK., Mum! Coming!
MOTHER Put that paper away, John. Dinner's ready.
FATHER Hmm.
JAMES [ENTERING] Liverpool's won the match, Dad—on a penalty.
FATHER Hmm.
MOTHER Janet came round with those holiday brochures, John. We need to make our decision soon.
FATHER Hmm.
JAMES Mum, did you tell Dad about my school report?
MOTHER [ENTHUSED] No, dear, I thought you should tell him.
JAMES Well...Dad—

[THE PHONE RINGS]

MOTHER I'll get it. Hello? Oh!...yes, he's right here.

[SHE HOVERS IN THE BACKGROUND, AS JAMES TRIES TO CONTINUE]

JAMES Anyway, Dad, I thought you'd be happy to hear that I got all four...
MOTHER [HANDING HIM THE PHONE] It's for you, John.
FATHER Oh! [BEAT] Hello? [VERY ANIMATED] Oh!—hello, Reggie! Good of you to call. About the Uniflex stock, I suggest you hold them until they peak at about...oh, 240, then sell the lot.

[VOICE TO BACKGROUND] The 'Dow' is down how many points? Unbelievable! Keep a close watch on that then. Tell me—how's the cashflow situation with you?

JAMES Look at him, Mum. He's alive again.

MOTHER Yes...maybe *we* should phone him.

[THEY FREEZE IN POSITION AS THE DISCUSSION LEADER ENTERS. AFTER A MOMENT, THEY EXIT]

THE QUESTIONS

1. Is there anything about this sketch that is familiar with your life at home? Does the father resemble anyone in your household? Who? How does that person make you feel?

2. What was it about the phone-call that seemed to bring the father 'to life'? Allowing for generalisations, do you think that most men are like the father in the sketch? Why? What is it about work that sparks a man's interest?

3. Do you think the father is right to behave the way he does towards his family? What would you suggest he should do to change? Is there anything his wife or son could do to help him—to draw him more into their family experience?

4. This father comes to you for counsel and advice about his family life. He thinks it's boring and monotonous. How would you help him?

CONFIDENCE

(Adapted with permission from CARE for the Family's *Family Matters*)

THE TOPIC/THEME
Self-esteem

THE SITUATION
A young man is passed over for a position and refuses to challenge the choice.

THE CHARACTERS
DAVID'S MOTHER
DAVID

THE PLACE
A home.

THE SKETCH

[DAVID ENTERS, VERY SUBDUED, PUTS DOWN BOOKS AND TAKES OFF COAT AS HIS MOTHER ENTERS FROM THE OPPOSITE SIDE AND GREETS HIM CHEERFULLY]

MOTHER Hello, David. It's about time you got home. Your father called. He'll be late again. We'll go on and eat without him. How was your day?

DAVID It was okay. We had a school paper committee meeting after school. They named the editors and staff.

MOTHER [REALISING THE SIGNIFICANCE] Ah! And?

DAVID They made Bill Whitely the editor.

MOTHER [SURPRISED] Bill Whitely? Norma Whitely's son? Why did they give it to him?

DAVID [SHRUGS] Heck if I know. They didn't consult with me.

MOTHER Oh, David—*you* should've been made editor! You're the most talented writer in your class!

DAVID It was their decision. It's not like there's anything I can do about it.

MOTHER Didn't you ask someone? There must be a *reason* they didn't pick you! Maybe I should call Mrs Lockler.

DAVID [REACTING] No. Mum! Don't! It's no use. Bill Whitely will do a good job. Probably better than me.

MOTHER Why do you say that? You're far more talented, the kids like you better—[PAUSE] David, why does this always happen to you? Why do you let people get away with it?— There's nothing wrong with asserting yourself when you can do a good job!

DAVID [SHRUGS] I...I just don't like to make a scene.

[THEY FREEZE IN POSITION AS THE GROUP LEADER ENTERS. THEN THEY EXIT]

THE QUESTIONS

1. What is David's biggest problem in this scene? If you were David, how would you handle being passed over for something you were qualified to do? David didn't want to 'make a scene'. Is it possible to assert yourself confidently without causing trouble? If so, how?

2. What causes a lack of self-confidence? Have you ever struggled with confidence? If so, under what circumstances? If not, how do you maintain your confidence?

3. Hebrews 11 presents a list of men and women in the Bible who were commended for their faith, yet a study of their lives shows times of doubt and what we might call a lack of confidence in their own abilities. Can you recall (or show from the Bible) how these various characters overcame their lack of confidence? Now read 2 Corinthians 3:4–6. What was the apostle Paul's thoughts on the subject? How can you apply his thinking to your own life?

DOWN FROM THE MOUNTAIN-TOP

THE TOPIC/THEME

Sensitivity

THE SITUATION

A troubled Christian seeks help from another Christian who is fresh from a spiritual experience.

THE CHARACTERS

FIRST PERSON

SECOND PERSON

THE PLACE

Wherever two people would feel comfortable talking.

THE SKETCH

[TWO FRIENDS ARE SITTING AS IF READY FOR A SERIOUS CONVERSATION. ONE IS LOOKING TROUBLED, THE OTHER IS BURSTING WITH NEW-FOUND SPIRITUAL JOY AFTER A WEEK AT A CHRISTIAN FESTIVAL]

TWO So—how are you? You sounded rather low on the phone.

ONE [WITH DIFFICULTY] It hasn't been a good week. I've been doing a lot of thinking and—

TWO I wish you had come with us to Green Harvest. What an experience!

ONE I'm sure it was. But, you see—

TWO We shook the ground, let me tell you. We praised through tongues and music. I've never felt anything like it.

ONE I'm glad you were able to go. However, I was—

TWO I thought of you quite a number of times. I kept thinking to myself, *everybody* should be in on this. You can't look at life the same way after you've been to Green Harvest. It puts things into proper perspective.

ONE Perspective. That's what I've been struggling with.

TWO That's what they taught about, you know. Perspective. Trying to see things as God sees them. The world, people in need...being sensitive in a spiritual way. I could show you my notes from the seminars.

ONE I'd like to see them. I've been having a lot of doubts, too, you see and—

TWO Doubts—we talked about that. Though it was hard to concentrate on trivial things like doubt when we were witnessing miracles of healing and receiving words of knowledge...It was absolutely amazing.

ONE I wish I could've seen it.

TWO You should have gone. Why didn't you?

ONE My mum's in the hospital.

TWO Oh, too bad. Maybe next year, then.

ONE Maybe.

TWO 'Cause it'll pick you right up and put your mind back in the proper perspective. Then you'll realise how mundane our little worries really are.

ONE Yeah...right.

TWO It was lovely talking to you. I'd better go now. [STANDS] We're having a get-together for those who went to 'Green Harvest'. Just to share in what we learned. [MOVES TO EXIT] Take care. [EXITS]

ONE Yeah...nice talking to you. [GETS UP DEJECTEDLY AND EXITS]

THE QUESTIONS

1. What was wrong with the communication between the two characters in this sketch?

2. Was the enthusiastic Christian a particularly sensitive listener?

3. How do you think the downtrodden Christian felt? Do you think he/she was uplifted by the enthusiastic Christian's experiences at 'Green Harvest'?

4. What are the dangers with Christians who have a 'Green Harvest' experience then return to normal living—and those who didn't share the experience?

GIFTS

THE TOPIC/THEME

Spiritual gifts

THE SITUATION

Two people talk about ways to get closer to God.

THE CHARACTERS

FIRST PERSON (in need of help)
SECOND PERSON (believes he/she has the answer)

THE PLACE

A home.

THE SKETCH

[BOTH PEOPLE ENTER CASUALLY, AS IF THEY'VE BEEN STROLLING AND TALKING. THEY SIT DOWN, FACING EACH OTHER]

SECOND PERSON I'm sorry you're so frustrated.

FIRST PERSON It helps to be able to talk about it. I...I want to be closer to God, but it's so difficult sometimes.

SECOND PERSON I think I know what'll help you.

FIRST PERSON Do you?

SECOND PERSON Yeah. Have you ever been slapped in the Spirit?

FIRST PERSON What?

SECOND PERSON Slapped in the Spirit!

FIRST PERSON I've never heard of such a thing.

SECOND PERSON I thought not. That's what you're missing. How can you expect to feel the power of God in your life when you haven't been slapped in the Spirit?

FIRST PERSON I don't understand this 'slapped' bit. You mean, somebody whacks me across the face or something?

SECOND PERSON Don't be silly! It's a spiritual surge, a renewal. You pray for God to slap you in the Spirit. It's incredible.

FIRST PERSON It would have to be. Okay, so let's say I do this...what happens next?

SECOND PERSON Then you sleep in thongs!

FIRST PERSON What?

SECOND PERSON Sleep in thongs.

FIRST PERSON Thongs?

SECOND PERSON You know, leather thongs? You've never felt anything like it.

FIRST PERSON	I'm sure. You mean, every night I have to—
SECOND PERSON	Not just every night. Whenever you need a spiritual pick-me-up. It's pretty basic.
FIRST PERSON	Sounds bizarre. 'Slapped in the Spirit', 'Sleeping in thongs'...
SECOND PERSON	Oh, that's not all. You'll also get to share verbs of knowledge.
FIRST PERSON	*What?* You're pulling my leg!
SECOND PERSON	Of course not. Only the elders can do that.
FIRST PERSON	Verbs of knowledge?
SECOND PERSON	Yeah—real action words. You get them supernaturally when you least expect it.
FIRST PERSON	And then?
SECOND PERSON	Then you tell the verb to the person it's directed to.
FIRST PERSON	This sounds so unbelievable. I don't remember anything about these things in the Bible.
SECOND PERSON	They're implied. Haven't you ever read first and second Carpathians?
FIRST PERSON	No.
SECOND PERSON	It's all there.
FIRST PERSON	[PONDERING THE IDEA] And I'll really be more spiritual?
SECOND PERSON	Of course.
FIRST PERSON	I'd like to think about it first.
SECOND PERSON	It doesn't work very well if you do that. God wants you to use your heart, not your brain.
FIRST PERSON	Really?
SECOND PERSON	Yeah. So—why don't we pray together now?
FIRST PERSON	Um, okay.
SECOND PERSON	[STANDING] Then let's go.
FIRST PERSON	Go? I thought we were going to—

SECOND PERSON	We are. But we need to go out to the kitchen to get some skillets!
FIRST PERSON	Skillets!
SECOND PERSON	Yeah! For the Laying on of Pans!

[FIRST PERSON EXITS. SECOND PERSON, BEWILDERED, EXITS. DISCUSSION LEADER ENTERS]

THE QUESTIONS

1. In the desire to become more intimate with God, many people suggest special methods or spiritual endowments to do it. Have you ever encountered any of these methods or 'gifts'? What were they? Did you feel closer to God as a result?

2. Read 1 Corinthians 12:1–11; 27–31 and 14. What are the various manifestations of the spirit Paul writes about? To whom are these manifestations given? Should every Christian expect to show these manifestations? What are the purposes of these manifestations?

3. Is there a connection between spiritual gifts and intimacy with God? Is it possible to manifest the gifts of the spirit and still feel distant from God? Read Matthew 7:21–23. What does this tell you about spiritual gifts and closeness to God?

4. According to John 14:23; 15:10 and Philippians 4:9 what is the best way to be close to God?

BORED

(Adapted with permission from CARE for the Family's *Family Matters*)

THE TOPIC/THEME

Staying at home.

THE SITUATION

Connie and Suzie have lunch together and catch up on their lives.

THE CHARACTERS

CONNIE (Dissatisfied housewife)
SUZIE (Enthused and envious of Connie's housewife status)

THE PLACE

A restaurant. (Two chairs and a small table could accomplish this effect, or you may elaborate as much as time and resources allow.)

THE SKETCH

[CONNIE AND SUZIE MIME AS IF THEY'VE JUST ORDERED THEIR FOOD]

CONNIE It's good to see you, Suzie. I don't often go out for lunch now.

SUZIE It's no wonder, now that you're a [PROUDLY] *housewife.*

CONNIE [NON-COMMITTAL] Yes... [BEAT] How are things at the office?

SUZIE Oh, the same. They still haven't replaced you, you know.

CONNIE Really?

SUZIE Gordon says he's going to threaten you to come back. I told him you wouldn't dream of it. 'She's the happy housewife', I said. 'Why would she want to come back to a dump like this?'

CONNIE What did Gordon say?

SUZIE He just grumbles and gripes, as usual. Oh, what I wouldn't give to be in your shoes... a loving husband, a beautiful home... what a life! It sure beats working for a living.

CONNIE Maybe I should talk to Gordon.

SUZIE What? Talk to Gordon? Why?

CONNIE My old job.

SUZIE What about your old job?

CONNIE Maybe I'll take it back.

SUZIE Are you mad? Why would you do a thing like that? I thought you enjoyed being home all day!

CONNIE I did. Everyone said it would be wonderful.

SUZIE So what's the matter?

CONNIE I'm bored.

[THEY FREEZE IN POSITION AS THE DISCUSSION LEADER STEPS FORWARD. AFTER A SUITABLE TIME, THEY EXIT]

THE QUESTIONS

1. Suzie is clearly envious of Connie because of how what she perceives Connie's life to be like. Put yourself in Suzie's mind and describe the life she believes Connie leads. Now describe, in your own words, your perception of the 'life of a housewife'.

2. Ask the women in your group who work at home to describe their lives. Do they like working at home? What are the most satisfying aspects of being a 'housewife'? What do they find least satisfying?

3. Connie is thinking about taking her old job back because she's bored. Do you think housewives are often bored at home? Again, survey the women in your group who can answer this question from experience. How can women keep from being bored at home? How can *mothers* keep from being bored at home?

4. What other adjustments do women have to make when they give up full-time work or careers to work at home?

THE SIXTIES

THE TOPIC/THEME
The Sixties and their effect on this generation

THE SITUATION
A daughter is ready for a Sixties fancy dress party and talks to her father about it.

THE CHARACTERS
JOHN (the father)
ALISON (his daughter)
MARY (the mother)

THE PLACE
A home.

THE SKETCH

[JOHN IS SITTING, READING THE NEWSPAPER. ALISON ENTERS. SHE IS WEARING SANDALS, BELL-BOTTOMS, PAISLEY SHIRT WITH UNMATCHING TURTLENECK, SUNGLASSES AND HEAD-BAND]

ALISON Peace, man.

JOHN [LOOKS UP, SURPRISED] Alison? Is that you or am I having a flashback?

ALISON It's me, Daddy. Like... right on.

JOHN Explain?

ALISON It's a sixties celebration party. Groovy, huh?

JOHN Do you have any idea how silly you look?

ALISON Silly! These are some cool threads, man. Do you know how hard it was to find these things?

JOHN Why?... have they started putting locks on the Oxfam rubbish bins?

ALISON Careful, Dad, you're sounding very establishment. We're going to remember a time when everyone was free-spirited and got tuned in and dropped out and grooved to the Beatles and the Rolling Stones and... [BEAT] You don't like it?

JOHN Sorry, I'm not as romantic about the Sixties as everyone else these days.

ALISON What was wrong with them? I think they were happening.

JOHN Trust me, it wasn't as good as everyone says it was. I was there, you weren't.

ALISON Then why are you so critical?

JOHN You really want to know? Because all the great ideas we had *then* have everything to do with the problems we're dealing with *now*. 'Get high', 'if it feels good, do it', 'Free love'. Not only did it wreck *my* generation, but it ruined yours as well. Nothing's free. Everything has a price-tag. That's what they forgot to mention.

ALISON But...but they still had some good ideas back then.

JOHN Good ideas, right. But, do you want to know something? They were *wrong*, OK.? They *sounded* good in the songs, but they didn't work—not in this world. Those ideas forgot something—that we're self-centred creatures who can't find love and peace on our own.

ALISON We should get you a box in Hyde Park.

JOHN See, the thing nobody seems to want to admit is that the ideas of the sixties *failed*. We didn't help the world. We didn't change anything. In fact, we made it worse. We wanted freedom without responsibility. And now the consequences are two decades of selfishness, drug epidemics, abortion on demand and AIDS.

ALISON But you can't just blame the sixties—an entire decade—for our problems.

JOHN I don't blame the sixties. I blame myself—because this thing we call the sixties was made up of people like me who got everything wrong.

ALISON Well, thanks for ruining a perfectly good party.

JOHN That's what you get for asking. [BEAT, AMUSED] Has your mother seen you like this? She won't believe it.

[MARY ENTERS DRESSED MUCH THE SAME AS HER DAUGHTER—EXCEPT SHE HAS ON A LEATHER VEST AND A TIE-DYE T-SHIRT]

MARY Let's go, Alison, we're going to be late.

ALISON Right.

MARY Come on, John—you can drive us.

JOHN What?

MARY Don't be a spoilsport.

[MARY AND ALISON EXIT]

JOHN [AMAZED] I hope we don't get arrested!

[HE EXITS AS THE DISCUSSION LEADER ENTERS]

THE QUESTIONS

1. What are your impressions of the sixties?

2. Do you agree or disagree with the father's attitudes about the sixties? Explain your answer.

3. What good came from the various social revolutions in the sixties?

4. Was there anything that happened in the sixties that you wish hadn't?

5. Many believe the sixties were responsible for the downfall of the church as a major influence in our society. Do you agree or disagree? Explain your answer. How could the church have been more responsive—whilst maintaining its spiritual integrity—to the needs of young people in the sixties?

NO TIME

(Adapted with permission of CARE for the Family's *Family Matters*)

THE TOPIC/THEME
Time/Busyness

THE SITUATION
A husband and wife don't have time to talk.

THE CHARACTERS
ELIZABETH
PATRICK

THE PLACE
A home.

THE SKETCH

[PATRICK IS IN A CHAIR, ELIZABETH ENTERS, RACING TO THE FRONT DOOR]

ELIZABETH See you later, love.
PATRICK Hang on! Where are you off to now?
ELIZABETH Meeting with a client. I won't be long.
PATRICK A client! Liz, it's past six.
ELIZABETH I know. But she's leaving for the city first thing in the morning.
PATRICK But I need to talk to you. We've hardly spoken all week.
ELIZABETH We'll talk when I get back.
PATRICK But I won't be here when you get back, I've got a meeting with Peter and Terry! They're in for the conference.
ELIZABETH Then we'll talk after *your* meeting.
PATRICK It's a late one. You'll be asleep.
ELIZABETH Really, Patrick, I have to go or I'll be late.
PATRICK When can we talk?
ELIZABETH [GETTING IMPATIENT] I don't know—we'll have to see!
PATRICK This isn't working, Elizabeth.
ELIZABETH [EXASPERATED] Can it *please* wait until I have time. I can't miss this meeting. Please?
PATRICK Oh...all right, go on then.

[SHE EXITS]

PATRICK [SIGHS] I'll make an appointment with your secretary.

[HE EXITS THE OPPOSITE DIRECTION AS THE DISCUSSION LEADER ENTERS]

THE QUESTIONS

1. Does this couple's dilemma resemble your own time pressure? If so, how?

2. Do you and your spouse have enough time together? If your answer is no, why not? Where does the time go? What efforts do you and your spouse make to manage time?

3. Do you wish you could slow down? What's stopping you? What might you have to change in your schedule and priorities to make more time for your spouse? Are you willing to do that?

4. If this sketch doesn't apply to you, explain how you and your spouse manage your schedule so you have time to yourselves.

5. Come up with a plan to insure time alone this week—*without* interruption.

TITHES

THE TOPIC/THEME
Tithing

THE SITUATION
Richard reacts to a preacher's appeal for money.

THE CHARACTERS
RICHARD
ANNE

THE PLACE
A home.

THE SKETCH

[RICHARD AND ANNE ARRIVE HOME FROM CHURCH. RICHARD IS ANGRY]

RICHARD That cheeses me off... it really does... why do they always have to preach about money?

ANNE Always? That's the first time I've ever heard David preach about money.

RICHARD Well... yes... and it was one time too many as far as I'm concerned.

ANNE But the church needs money.

RICHARD Who doesn't?

ANNE Now, Richard...

RICHARD Doesn't he think *we* have bills?

ANNE I'm sure he knows that...

RICHARD Perhaps he thinks I work all week just so I can turn around and give all my money to the church, is that it?

ANNE Richard, we barely give anything *now*.

RICHARD It puts me off, that's all. When they start talking about money, I want to put locks on my wallet!

ANNE The Bible says that God loves a cheerful giver.

RICHARD Who can be cheerful with David ramming the need for money down my throat?

ANNE It was hardly ramming. In fact, it was hardly a suggestion. He simply said...

RICHARD I know what he said. Every word. I know the pattern, that's all. He starts talking about money this Sunday and *next* Sunday he'll expect us to get *involved*. It's always the same.

ANNE We've been going to this church for three years. Don't you think we *should* be involved?

RICHARD All I know is if this keeps up, we're going somewhere else. I don't go to church to be pressurised. Do you hear me? We're going to another church if he doesn't stop. [STORMS OFF]

ANNE [SIGHS] Yes, Richard. Just like the last time. [SHE FOLLOWS HIM OFF]

THE QUESTIONS

1. Do you agree with Richard's feelings? Why or why not?

2. Do you tithe regularly? Why or why not?

3. Consider the following verses from the Bible: Luke 6:38; Malachi 3:8; 2 Corinthians 9:6 and Matthew 6:21. What do these verses teach about giving to God?

WHAT'S THE MATTER WITH DAD?

(Adapted with permission of CARE for the Family's *Family Matters*)

THE TOPIC/THEME
Unemployment

THE SITUATION
Two young people talk about their father's unemployment.

THE CHARACTERS
TOM
PAMELA

THE PLACE
A young man's room.

THE SKETCH

[A SON IS IN HIS BEDROOM LISTENING TO THE STEREO. HIS SISTER ENTERS AND TURNS IT OFF]

TOM Hey! I was listening to that!

PAMELA Dad wants you downstairs.

TOM [EXASPERATED] What now?

PAMELA I don't know. But you want to watch yourself. He's in a mood.

TOM He and mum have another row?

PAMELA No.

TOM [SUSPICIOUSLY] What did you do?

PAMELA I didn't do anything. Hurry up.

TOM What, then? I'm not going down without knowing.

PAMELA I'm not sure. He went to sign on and was angry when he got back.

TOM [REALISING] That's it—he had to sign on.

PAMELA What?

TOM The dole. He gets moody when he has to sign on. Haven't you noticed?

PAMELA Why's it such a big deal to him?

TOM Likes to work for his money, I s'pose. Bit old-fashioned. It doesn't make a lot of sense to me.

PAMELA Not much does.

TOM Thanks!

PAMELA Go on. He's probably fuming.

TOM I don't know why it bothers him so much. I mean...it was only a job.

[THEY EXIT AS THE DISCUSSION LEADER ENTERS]

THE QUESTIONS

1. Tom establishes the connection between his father's bad moods and having to sign on—yet he's bewildered about why it would bother his father so much. Why do you think Tom's father is upset?

2. Do you think there is a relationship between a man's self-esteem and his work? Explain your answer.

3. What do you think happens to a man who has been unemployed for a long time?

4. Have you ever been unemployed? When? How long did it last? How did you feel? Did those around you understand the effect it was having on you? What was the outcome?

5. Should the church have a programme to help the unemployed? If so, suggest ways to start one.

GUILTY

(Adapted with permission from CARE for the Family's *Family Matters*)

THE TOPIC/THEME
Unnecessary guilt

THE SITUATION
A woman discusses her feelings about her separation from her husband.

THE CHARACTERS
WIFE (Judith)
NEIGHBOUR (Elaine)

THE PLACE
Judith's home.

THE SKETCH

[A HOME. A COUPLE OF NEIGHBOURS (TWO WOMEN ACTUALLY) FINISHING TEA]

WIFE I don't know what happened, Elaine. I thought everything was fine and suddenly—he's gone.

NEIGHBOUR I'm sorry, Judith. You've got to face it. He was a swine...an absolute swine.

WIFE I tried to be a good wife.

NEIGHBOUR You slaved over him hand-and-foot. He didn't deserve you.

WIFE I worked hard to keep our marriage together...even when he said he was leaving I held on.

NEIGHBOUR He had a roving eye for anything in a skirt. Everyone knew it, but we didn't know how to tell you.

WIFE I thought I was a good lover. He certainly never complained.

NEIGHBOUR He wouldn't know a commitment if it grabbed him by the throat.

WIFE In everything, I never stopped loving him.

NEIGHBOUR He doesn't know the meaning of the word.

WIFE You say all that and...I know it must be true. But I can't get rid of this feeling.

NEIGHBOUR What feeling?

WIFE I feel guilty.

NEIGHBOUR *You* feel guilty!

WIFE Yes...I can't get rid of this feeling that I did something wrong.

[THEY FREEZE IN POSITION. THE DISCUSSION LEADER ENTERS AND, IN A TIMELY MANNER, THEY EXIT]

THE QUESTIONS

1. It is clear from the neighbour's comments that Judith's husband was a real rat-bag. Yet, Judith feels guilty—as if *she* had done something wrong—about their separation. Why?

2. Have you ever felt guilty for something that wasn't your fault? How did you reconcile those feelings with the facts? Where do those guilty feelings come from?

3. Is guilt ever healthy? If so, when?

4. Read Romans 5:1; 8:1; 30; 34; Hebrews 10:17; 1 John 1:9; 2:1 and Jeremiah 33:8. What do these verses tell you about confessed sin and guilt?